GROWING UP AND GROWING OLD IN APPALACHIAN KENTUCKY

Benny Ray Bailey, Ph.D
Nikki Rieck Bailey

CorKenWyaKasEmm Publishing

Published by CorKenWyaKasEmm Publishing
ISBN: 978-0-692-87851-4
Card Catalogue Number: 2017940544
Growing Up and Growing Old in Appalachian Kentucky |
Benny Ray Bailey, Ph.D and Nikki Rieck Bailey
Digital distribution | CorKenWyaKasEmm Publishing
Paperback | CorKenWyaKasEmm Publishing, 2017

DEDICATION

For Nikki, Viola Tackett Bailey,
Malcolm Glenn, Benny Ray,
Chet Daniel,
Rebekah Dereath,
Steven Paul, Courtney Nicole,
Kennedy Michele,
Wyatt Benjamin,
Kashlynn Monroe, and
Emmett Morrison Bailey.

TABLE OF CONTENTS

CHAPTER ONE

INTRODUCTION

Benny Ray Bailey was born in 1944 in the community of Price, on Left Beaver Creek, in Floyd County, Kentucky. Floyd County, Kentucky, founded in 1799, is situated about 130 miles east of Lexington, in the center of Appalachia. While he would go on to bring advanced medical resources to his region, he was delivered at home by a lay mid wife, like most children in this part of the country at that time. For the first ten to fifteen years of his life, his world consisted of how far away from home he could walk in the morning, and get back before dark.

Any tale about Benny Ray Bailey quickly becomes intertwined with the history of Appalachia, the region he spent his life dedicated to preserving and defending. Bailey remembers the mountain landscape of his youth as a site of endless possibility, recalling that, "When you got in the hills, or anywhere out of sight of home, you could be anywhere or anybody you wanted. The only restriction were the restrictions you put on yourself. You could be rich, famous, a professional athlete, anything you could dream of, you could be."

By the time Bailey was growing up in Appalachia, her people had been historically poor to the extent that they were leaving the region at alarming rates, to find work. While many stories about Appalachians become tragedies of choosing between the home you love and finding success, Benny Ray Bailey's story is the opposite of that. Instead of leaving his hometown for Columbus or Lexington or New York or Chicago, he left for the next county over, and spent his life dedicated to proving wrong anyone who would assert that you couldn't make a living or find a way to contribute in Appalachia outside the coal industry.

At twenty-two, Benny Ray Bailey was creating jobs for himself, because of the simple fact that no one had come along before him with the idea to do the things he wanted to do. He worked as a teacher, an educational administrator, a fundraiser, a founder of the first advanced health facilities in his region, and a state senator who was willing to stand up to the coal industry to establish the first means by which the people of Kentucky were fairly compensated for their land in the history of that industry in that region. Benny Ray did all this in a culture that told him that to have a full and successful life, he needed to move as far away as he could from the mountains.

The Appalachian Mountains that bore up Benny Ray Bailey are the oldest mountain range in the world, and the Appalachian people are among the oldest groups of non-native people to inhabit the continental United States. Bailey writes, "History tells us the Rocky Mountains have risen and fallen twice while the Appalachian still stood. During the two great Ice Ages, which covered the globe, only the peaks of the mighty Appalachians stood above the ice. As the ice retreated, the seeds and saplings of these Appalachian Mountains receded with the ice and replenished the globe. Today, you can find relatives of the chestnut, oak and elm trees of Appalachia as far away as China. Not only that, but there are more different types of vegetation growing in the Appalachian Mountains than on any other part of the globe."

Thus began the tradition of the Appalachian Mountains spreading their resources all across the earth, whether it be the seeds of trees to China or their best and brightest citizens to New York or Chicago. The natural resources are sent away too, to power homes and offices and businesses all across the United States and the world. For as long as she has been powering the country with her resources, Appalachia has been known as poor and backward—and indeed, this reputation aided and abetted those who wanted to pillage the region. Bailey remarks that he "got the same introduction to my culture as everyone else. We were studied, restudied, discovered and forgotten, analyzed and re-analyzed, praised and pitied. Appalachians seemed to agree that there was a different world somewhere, and that this different world was better than anything we had or were accustomed to. I believed this, as it was the only thing we were taught."

About ninety-four percent of people born in Appalachia in the earlier part of the twentieth century were descendants of those who lived on the border of the region during the Revolutionary War, making Appalachians almost half the living descendants of the first colonial Americans. Three quarters of the people who settled Appalachia were Scotch- Irish, a majority of whom spoke a Northern dialect of English about a hundred years older than the English of Shakespeare. By the 1760's, the Governor of North Carolina observed that each year at least 1000 wagons of Scotch-Irish immigrants traveled through Salisbury, North Carolina, to settle in the mountains.

When the Revolutionary War started, eighty-percent of the inhabitants of the eastern border of Appalachia were Scotch-Irish. This population, who had moved around the globe to escape the shabby treatment of the British government, sided with the Colonists against the British in the Revolutionary War. One group of Scotch-Irish Appalachians prevailed at the Battle of King's Mountain on October 7, 1790, where they roundly defeated the British, paving the way for the surrender at Yorktown. After they won the battle, the Appalachian soldiers returned to the mountains, hanging their prisoners along the way. Today there is still a row of Tory Oak trees that leads from King's Mountain into the mountains. As Benny says, "they killed one British soldier for every shot."

This group of immigrants represents the largest group of educated people to settle the early United States, starting in the early 1700s. They came mostly from Northern Ireland, where they had been forced to move to practice John Knox's radical interpretations of Calvinism. Part of their fundamental doctrine was that all men were sinners, and that everyone was responsible for their own exploration of truth. To equip each sinner for this mission, the Church taught that every child should learn to "read, write, and cipher" --an earlier version of the classic three R's, "reading, writing, and arithmetic". In Northern Ireland, Knox's followers had founded some of the first schools to educate both boys and girls. The first settlers of Appalachia brought these practices and values to the United States, and their schools became models for the entire system of American public education. Many of the first Appalachians were among the first working class literate Americans; often they paid their way to America by tutoring the children of the wealthy, as indentured servants, molding such influential minds as James Madison and Thomas Jefferson. In fact, according to U S News, these "hill people," have furnished more Presidents of the United States, 7 (seven), than any other recognizable immigrant group.

The first Appalachians built churches immediately upon settling in the mountains, and shortly thereafter built schools associated with the churches, where the children learned to read (especially the Bible), write, and cipher. Appalachia maintained a high literacy rate until the Civil War, during which the schools had to close because of the extent of violence that erupted between Union and Confederate sympathizers. Most Appalachians sided with the Union, especially because there was no use for slavery in the majority of Appalachia, where the geography prevented large scale, plantation-style farming. However, every area of Appalachia was divided, in the most literal version of the brother against brother, neighbor against neighbor warfare that exemplified the tragedy of the Civil War. During the Civil War, the schools in Appalachia closed for a generation to protect children and teachers from violence. In 1890, the school year in Pike County, Kentucky, was four months long and attendance averaged 20 per cent.

When the schools in Appalachia re- opened, they were not established by the people of Appalachia and organized around their churches, they were built by Northern churches, who regarded the mountain people as wholly different from themselves. This is when the word "Appalachian" is first used in popular culture, to distinguish the Appalachians as those Americans not from the North or the South. After the Union victory over the South, Northern churches began to send leaders and teachers to the mountains to "educate" the Appalachians. The Appalachians still spoke a version of English descended from their Scotch- Irish ancestors, but their dialect was ridiculed by visitors from the North, who pressured Appalachians to learn "proper" English. Outsiders also considered Appalachian religious rituals, musical traditions to be backward and foreign, though most of these practices (like chanting) were long accepted in Europe, especially among European royalty.

The efforts by Northerners to "civilize" Appalachians relied on of a long tradition of negatively stigmatizing Appalachians, continuing through television shows like Green Acres or Hee-Haw, until, as Bailey says, "We went through generations laughing at everything that was our own until we became a very self-conscious people. We felt that anybody, anywhere, was better than we, that we were among the most worthless people in the world."

The English treatment of the Scotch-Irish, the chaotic, divisive violence of the Civil War, which, to most Appalachians, was based on an argument between far away powers that did not affect them, was followed by the rule of the coal industry. By the middle of the twentieth century, when Benny Ray Bailey was born, Appalachia, particularly eastern Kentucky, was entirely dominated by an industry which plundered the resources of the region while providing little to no compensation or support to the people who owned and lived on the land. Bailey likes to point out that "the largest gathering of financiers ever assembled wasn't on Wall Street—it was in Jenkins, Kentucky. John Rockefeller, John Jacob Astor, Jay Gould, and others met there to divvy up the Appalachia mineral fields."

Benny Ray Bailey's grandmother was married at the age of seventeen. The night her husband, Ben, spent in the funeral home was their first night apart since their marriage. Bailey's father, who later worked as a coal miner, was in the army when he was born, so Bailey spent a great deal of time with his maternal grandparents, Ben and Martha Tackett. His mother, the fifth child of 10, had 7 sisters, Ella, Mellie, Mary, Hannah, Fannie, Cora and Mae, and 2 brothers, Jim and Curt. Cora and Mae were still single when Bailey was born, and they spent a great deal of time caring for him when he was a young child. Bailey was very close to all his aunts and uncles, but especially Cora and Mae, who doted on him; Bailey says, "they were petting on me when I was a baby, and they were petting on me till they died!"

The family had radio at home, but didn't have television until the late fifties, when Bailey was eleven or twelve years old. Television reception was very bad, and the only channel that the family could watch was WSAZ, of Huntington, West Virginia. To get this station, a television line and two wires had to be strung from the house to the mountaintop about a mile away, where there was an antenna set up on the top of the mountain. All this trouble was worth it, Bailey recalls, because, "Television, when we were able to get reception, did give us a window to the outside world –but when it rained, there was no reception whatsoever."

While Bailey's mother valued education, no one ever considered that anyone in the family would be educated beyond high school. Bailey's sisters were both married before high school graduation, but they finished high school. His younger brother, Shannon, would go on to earn a B.S. and an M.S. at Morehead State College. Bailey had many friends in high school, as did everyone in the community, where, Benny says, "everyone knew everyone." He remembers spending time with Doug Mullins, Monty Hall, Ernie Paul Combs, Robert Griffith, Dean Stewart, Carson Akers, Dwayne Little, Doug Frazier, Roy Frazier, Freddy Hall, and many others. His mother was friends with all these boys' parents, so little was done that their parents didn't know about, which made it difficult to get into any real trouble. His family was also very religious, and his mother "kept us on a short leash." They were a very religious family; Bailey's grandmother told him that she joined the church when she was thirteen years old, when she married his grandfather. The family was Old Regular Baptist, a fundamentalist Christianity which followed John Calvin and John Knox, "believing that man is basically a sinner, so church discipline must be very strict."

Athletics were an encouraged and approved activity, provided by the coal industry as well as the school system. The Inland Steel Company, who built the town of Wheelwright, KY, and had mining operations in the area, founded the little league teams on upper Left Beaver Creek, from Price to Weeksbury. Bailey played little league baseball for five years, and his team won a tournament that featured teams from Left Beaver Creek and Pike County. Tommy Hall, who always assisted the teams, still had the trophy from this tournament when he died. Bailey tried to play high school basketball, and made the varsity team as a senior; however, he says that, "the benevolence and compassion of the coach, Pete Grigsby, Jr., had more to do with my making the team than my abilities. I was not a very good basketball player and I always thought very fondly of Coach Grigsby for giving me the opportunity to play."

Until second grade, Bailey attended a one room school house, in which six grades were educated in one room. After first grade, Bailey attended McDowell School in Frazier's Creek. Bailey recalls school being relatively easy, but he was not inspired to pursue good grades. He recalls that the emphasis in school had shifted from "reading, writing, and 'rithmatic," to "reading, writing, and the road to Columbus," --and perhaps it was this third point that stuck in Bailey's craw. While over a third of Appalachians have moved away from the area, Bailey has lived there his entire life ("Almost, but not yet," he'll remind you).

While in high school, Bailey worked in a service station on the weekends and during the summer. He worked twelve to fourteen hours a day, for five dollars a day. The son of a coal miner, he worked around coal mining, chopping trees and cutting wood to be used in the mines, or "making timbers," as early as ages fourteen and fifteen. He graduated thirty-second in a class of sixty-four, but didn't take much of an interest until senior year, when his father left the family, just as many of his friends and classmates were also leaving their hometown on that "road to Columbus." Bailey was the second youngest of five children; when his father left, Bailey's older sisters, Emogene and Aileen, had already married and left home, and his older brother, Doug, had left to join the Air Force. Bailey was sixteen when his father left, and his younger brother, Shannon, who he helped to parent and remained close to until Shannon's death in 2007. Bailey was always very close to his mother, but had little contact with his father after his father's departure when he was sixteen.

After his father left home, Bailey became more serious about his schoolwork, but his grades were not high enough to gain him admittance to college. He applied to a small junior college near his home called Caney Junior College, which became Alice Lloyd College. Alice Lloyd College allowed students to work their way through the program even if they couldn't afford tuition. Bailey had a very difficult time in gaining admission, but he received help from Dottie Howell, a student who worked in the administration offices. Dottie Howell was the niece of Adrian Howell, who was married to Bailey's aunt, Mae. Bailey says that, "Dottie had more to do with my acceptance into college than anyone."

Bailey remained close to his large, extended family, which at one point included seventy-six cousins within the county limits, through his adult life, when many of them worked on his campaigns for state senate. Bailey's childhood in the rural Kentucky mountains would not limit his exposure to the world, and in fact the pursuit of change for his own region would lead him all over the globe, to New York, San Francisco, Washington, D.C., and Chicago. Bailey's unflappable connection to his roots did not deter his ascent to political office, but inspired his political career to effect real change that was based on his intimate knowledge of Appalachia and her people.

Later, Bailey and his wife, Nikki Rieck, would go on to establish a scholarship at every public high school in Floyd and Knott Counties. In the same district where Bailey was once an uninspired student, he has returned many times over to provide motivation and inspiration to young people like himself. To anyone who might believe they must choose between their home and success, Benny Ray Bailey provides a counter example, leading those who come after him not with mere words, but by example.

CHAPTER TWO

A COMMITMENT TO THE APPALACHIAN REGION

Whenever Benny Ray, or his collaborator, Dr. Grady Stumbo, are asked why they were so motivated to stay in Appalachia, they immediately answered that their experience at Alice Lloyd College was what inspired them to spend their lives working to build up Appalachia, rather than moving away.

Today, Alice Lloyd College seems to have lost its vision and its purpose. While initially the college was part of a community center, many think that today the college seeks isolation from the communities it was founded to serve. Initially, the college was founded as a private institution, today it is the largest recipient of tax dollars for its students in the county. Although many believe it is the wealthiest institution in Knott County, the college receives millions of tax dollars in student aid each year. Despite seemingly abandoning its initial purposes, the college still offers an educational opportunity to students who quite possibly could not afford to attend alternate institutions.

When Bailey attended Alice Lloyd College, the school was called Caney Junior College. The school was founded by Alice Lloyd in 1916, as the Caney Creek Community Center. The college emerged as a division of the Community Center. Ms. Alice Geddes Lloyd, a Wellesley graduate originally from Boston, and her friend Ms. June Buchannan, founded many grade schools and several high schools in East Kentucky. Known for her philanthropy, Mrs. Lloyd was even featured on "This is Your Life" in 1955. The focus of her work was education without an interference with religion or politics; she especially encouraged people to stay in their local communities, to apply their education to the improvement of their whole community rather than simply improving their lives as individuals.

The goal at Alice Lloyd College, located in Pippa Passes, KY, was to provide a quality education to Appalachians, and to provide motivation and opportunity for them to apply their learning to staying in East Kentucky. Students paid just twenty dollars per semester at Alice Lloyd College, which covered tuition as well as room and board in the school's dormitory. Benny Ray recalls that, "you paid $20 if you had it; if you didn't, you didn't have to pay it." Students were also required to work on campus for one or two hours every day. Benny Ray points out, "the term 'dormitory' is used loosely: there was no running water or indoor plumbing." The school was Christian, but non-denominational. Alice Lloyd had made two promises to the community: not to interfere with politics or religion. However, today many observers believe the college has even violated these two founding principles.

Alice Lloyd College had a profound impact on Bailey's life. There were only two administrators

there, Will Hayes and Bill Hughes. Mr. Hughes
saw potential in Benny Ray and took an interest
in him. Hughes began to give Benny Ray more
and more responsibilities outside the classroom.
He made Bailey a dorm monitor, which they
called "house- fathers," and made him a student
work manager. Hughes told Bailey that he,
"didn't want to see him outside the dorm unless
he was going to class, going to work, or going to
eat." Bestowing these responsibilities and expectations on Bailey made Hughes the greatest influence on his life at this point. William R.
Hughes was an influential figure on campus for
many students; Benny Ray reflects, "I would
suspect there are others who attended Caney
that would make the same statement regarding
Mr. Hughes."

Alice Lloyd, or Caney Junior College, was very
strict at the time Benny Ray attended. Boys and
girls were not allowed to socialize, indeed, not
allowed to talk to each other. Boys had to wear
coats and ties to class and meals, while girls had
to wear white uniforms, with red ties. Bailey was
a "house father" which meant that he was in
charge of supervising other students, organizing
work schedules and generally bearing the re-
sponsibility of a young authority figure. Hughes
later reflected that Benny Ray "thought I was
trying to kill him, but he measured up with better than a 3.0 average and did a commendable
job both as a house parent and work manager."

In the summer of 1963, Benny Ray married his
high school sweetheart, Celestine Little, and by
1964 they had a baby, Malcolm Glenn. Celestine's parents, Malcolm and Beatrice Little, were

21

a substantial help to the young family during this time. They helped particularly by providing child-care for Malcolm Glenn, nicknamed "Bubby." Bubby was a special joy to Benny Ray, and to all of his family. Benny Ray remembers, "He was a typical boy, into everything, but especially smart. He loved anything to do with sports."

Benny Ray spent the spring and summers of the sixties playing fast pitch softball in the Floyd County League. The team was Price but there were also teams at Wheelwright, Weeksbury, McDowell, Dinwood, Allen, David, Ivel, Betsy Layne, Prater Creek, Harold, Garrett and Wayland. The players were pretty bad at the start because they could not find men who could pitch the fast pitch. After about 5 years, their pitcher, Sid Robinson, got the hang of throwing the ball under handed, and Benny Ray also learned to pitch. In 1966, Price won the Floyd County Softball league in a double elimination tournament. They defeated Weeksbury during the first game, 1-0; Weeksbury defeated them in the second game 2-1; they defeated Weeksbury in the third and final game 1-0. Many observers say this was the best softball tournament and best final series in the history of the Floyd County league. Their team consisted of Benny Ray, Babe Frazier, Doug Frazier, Danny Pennington, Malcolm Little, Bernard Little, Herman Mullins, Alvin Little, Alton Little, Bob Caudill, Jimmy Hopkins, and Sid Robinson. As with all civic and community improvements projects on Left Beaver Creek, Glenn "Greener" Fraizier was also involved and served as manager of the softball team. The softball team was a big part of the life in the community during the early 1960's, bringing adults in the community together outside of work, school, or religion.

Another important community project that Benny Ray was involved in was the creation of the Left Beaver Fire Department and Rescue Squad. Led, again by Glenn Frazier who served as Captain and aided by Malcolm Little, Doug Frazier, Harold Newman, T.J. Hagans, Alvin Little, Freddy Hall and others. The Left Beaver Rescue Squad became a focal point of the community and served as a gathering place for the community.

As was so common in Appalachia, the young Bailey family had to move from home to find work for periods of time. After graduating from Alice Lloyd in the summer of 1964, Benny Ray joined two of his sisters and many of his relatives in Detroit, where they had found jobs. Benny Ray was fortunate enough to find a job at a steel mill, Taylor Gaskin, which allowed him to work ten hours per day, seven days per week. While the mill only paid $1.70 per hour, they paid time and a half for all hours over forty per week, and double time for Sunday. Benny Ray went from having nothing to bringing home over $175 per week after taxes. At the end of the summer 1964, he had two checks, one for $1596 that he had saved, and his last paycheck for $136. He returned to Kentucky, gave the last paycheck to his mother, and set off to Pikeville College to complete his undergraduate education.

Pikeville College, in Pikeville, KY, was a private school founded by the Presbyterian Church.

There wasn't much financial aid available at this time, nor were there many available scholarships. Benny Ray did get a National Defense Student Loan of $300 per semester, and a limited college work study which paid $1 per hour for student work. Benny Ray went to Pikeville College for three semesters and one summer term, taking as many credits at a time as he could in order to graduate as quickly as possible. One semester, he took 24 semester hours at Pikeville, by taking Saturday classes.

By the time Benny Ray finished college, he was really broke. The U.S. Government, through the college student work program, had provided some employment during college – students earned $1 hour to clean dorms and public areas of the campus, and through the National Defense Student Loan, Bailey borrowed a total of $1100 to attend college. He repaid the loan in its entirety and, since then, has paid over one million dollars in taxes to state and local government. The government loaned him $1100, and got their money back plus $1 million. Unsurprisingly, Benny Ray Bailey turned out to be a pretty good investment.

Once he finished his degree, with a major in History and Political Science and a minor in German, Bailey got a job teaching at Prestonsburg High School. He finished college on January 28, 1966, and began teaching the following Monday. The teacher he was hired to replace had resigned in October, 1965, and the students had substitute teachers from October until the end of January. As a result, the history students had only studied three chapters in five months.

After a semester at Prestonsburg, Benny Ray was sent to Wheelwright High School for the 1966-1967 school year. Again, he was assigned to "sponsor" the senior class. At the age of twenty-two, he had students in class as old as he was. During this school year, it became apparent to Benny Ray that he could not live and raise a family on the salary of a public school teacher. In 1966-1967, he received a salary of $299 per month, hardly enough to provide for a growing family.

One of the county education supervisors, Hugo Miller, came to his classroom one day and gave him a booklet that listed federal programs that would pay experienced teachers to go to graduate school. Benny Ray applied for, and received, a fellowship to Indiana State University in Terre Haute, Indiana. This fellowship paid him a total of $6600 (tax free), paid his tuition to study for a Master's of Science in Guidance Counseling.

This money which paid Benny Ray to go to graduate school was more than double what he was paid to teach full time. He was off to Indiana State University.

Another interesting point about Benny Ray's time at Indiana State University. Benny Ray organized a slow pitch softball team which included all the participants in the Experienced Teacher Fellowship Program, along with much of the faculty. The team won the Terre Haute Slow Pitch Softball League in 1968.

In the summer of 1966, Benny Ray had worked in a community enrichment program funded by the Office of Economic Opportunity through Alice Lloyd College. He worked in the communities of Toler Creek and Prater Creek in Floyd County. This program provided outreach to local communities to address gaps in their basic medical and nutritional needs. Benny Ray thoroughly enjoyed this work and felt as though the program really helped the young people he worked with.

In the summer of 1967, Bill Hughes asked Benny Ray to return to Alice Lloyd College, to serve as Director of the Summer Program for the Leslie, Knott, Letcher and Perry Community Action Council. Benny Ray accepted the job, and really enjoyed this summer of running the program. As Benny Ray was finishing the MS program at Indiana State, he began to look for employment.

CHAPTER THREE

THE ALCOR PROGRAM

As he was completing the Masters of Science program at Indiana State, Benny Ray began to look for full-time employment. Having treasured his undergraduate experience at Alice Lloyd College, Benny Ray wrote a letter to Mr. Will Hayes, the college president, asking if there were positions available. Mr. Hayes called, and invited Benny Ray to campus for a job interview. Hayes offered the twenty-three-year-old a position as Assistant Dean of Students. The Dean of Students was Charlie Whitaker, who Benny Ray remembers as "one of the best people I had ever met," so he readily accepted the position.

At Alice Lloyd College, Benny Ray administered several programs for the college, as well as teaching classes to the students. He was also Director of Co-Op Education, Director of Admissions, and Director of Student Work Programs, as well as being Assistant Dean of Students and an instructor. One of the programs Benny Ray administered had begun with a few medical and nursing students who wanted to serve rural communities during their summers.

During this time, America was engaged in a "War on Poverty," which had been declared in Martin County, Kentucky, by President Johnson.

President Kennedy had created the Peace Corps in 1961, and Johnson's "poverty program," which later became AmeriCorps, was an attempt to provide Americans with an opportunity to do the same kind of work in America that the Peace Corps was doing overseas. Johnson's "War on Poverty" employed American volunteers in The Volunteers In Service To America program, or VISTA.

VISTA had a program for Appalachia, which paid volunteers $100 per month. However, the volunteers had to pay about $80 per month in room and board. Another program that sent college students into Appalachia, inner cities, and reservations, to work for the summer, paid students $180 per month, and students had to pay $100 per month for room and board. These programs effectively eliminated poor students from participating in them. This meant that the volunteers working with poorer populations had little if any experience of the under-privileged conditions under which the people they were helping lived. Students like Benny Ray, who worked during the summers to finance their educations, were forced to seek work "up North" so that they could return to school each fall, and were effectively priced out of volunteering.

While he worked at Alice Lloyd College (ALC), Benny Ray directed a program which helped Appalachian college students run summer programs for their fellow Appalachians. The program soon focused primarily on medical students and nursing students, giving them a way to apply their skills in the region. This program provided much needed basic medical care to many under-served communities. Initially, the program was funded by Office of Economic Opportunity (through the Federal government), hiring around fifty local college students to work in the summer in isolated communities for $75 per week. This allowed students to apply their skills locally, without having to move far away for summer employment.

In early 1969, Ms. Edith Friedman, Executive Director for the Bruner Foundation, and Mr. Martin Barrell, Chairman of the Board of the Bruner Foundation, from New York City, came by ALC looking for "student work programs" that their foundation could fund. Mr. Hayes asked Benny Ray to meet with them, and Benny Ray told them about the student programs he had directed in the past. As a result, the Bruner Foundation funded the ALC student work program, which was later called ALCOR (Alice Lloyd College Out Reach), for $350,000 over a three-year period. This was, at the time, the largest grant in the history of the college.

Mr. Hayes asked Benny Ray to direct the program, which he did. In 1969, ACLOR operated programs in sixteen communities in Leslie, Letcher, Knott, Perry and Floyd Counties. That year they were visited by officials of the Appalachian Regional Commission, who had a program attempting to recruit health care professionals to serve in the medically under-served areas of Appalachia. The Appalachian Regional Commission asked if ALCOR would be interested in placing student nurses in each community with the hope that these students would return to Appalachia after finishing their education. They agreed, and received funding to hire sixteen student nurses for the summer.

The Appalachian Regional Commission, a joint federal, state, and regional agency, was founded primarily as a road building agency, and had funded a program for the Student American Medical Association (SAMA) to bring medical, nursing, pharmacy, and dental students into Appalachia for summer work. The Director of this SAMA program was Grady Stumbo, a 2nd year medical student at the University of Kentucky. The odd thing was, Grady Stumbo was also a graduate of McDowell High School in Floyd County, and Alice Lloyd College. Benny Ray was one year ahead of Grady in school, but the two had known each other their entire lives.

Grady worked alongside Benny Ray in the ALCOR program in 1969 and, in 1970, they combined the ALCOR program with the SAMA program in Kentucky. Grady, now in his third year of medical school, directed the health aspect of the ALCOR program. While there were federal funds in ALCOR to pay the health care aspects of the program, all the remaining funds came from private foundations. In the summer of 1970, they added Cumberland College in Williamsburg, KY, Lees' College in Jackson, KY., and Southeast Community College in Cumberland, KY to the ALCOR program. At this time, they also changed the acronym of the program from Alice Lloyd Community Out Reach to Appalachian Leaders in Community Out Reach. They also formed a nationwide Board of Directors for ALCOR, and incorporated the program as a free standing, not for profit corporation.

In 1970, ALCOR directed seventy community centers in a total of twenty-two counties in East KY and East TN, and each center included a student health team. Each medical team provided medical, dental, and nutritional guidance to the communities they served. The goal was not to change the people, but to educate them about the basics of nutrition and healthcare, as well as attending to their immediate medical needs. Benny Ray told the Floyd County Times, "I tell these people all the time: Be proud you're from Eastern Kentucky. Be proud that you eat soup beans, they're good. Don't be ashamed that you like to crumble up cornbread in them, just because somebody with a different set of rules says it's bad manners. Don't be ashamed of liking country music. It's your own music, and something that belongs to you alone, has a special value for you. These are the most beautiful children on earth, right here in these hollows. They need to be fulfilled, not changed."

The focus of the work of ALCOR was community empowerment, as well as medical care. The ACLOR students would set up a community center, often times using the school building during the summer months. The community center was a place where children could go during the day to do educational and athletic activities, almost all of which included learning about health, nutrition, and hygiene.

At night, the adults could gather at the center to discuss parenting concerns and exchange wisdom as they learned rug hooking and other crafts, or just gathered to watch the children play, or share a meal. ALCOR would host a cookout and pay for them, but under the conditions that the parents of the children would come in to plan the menu. Benny Ray recalls, "We told the parents that we'd only pay for it if it was guaranteed to be nutritional, and here's why/how that works; we'd show them the food groups that have to be included in the meal, it was a kind of painless education." When the children would arrive at the centers in the morning, they could read, play, draw, and generally do whatever they wanted, as long as they brushed their teeth first. This, like many hygiene lessons, was made into a game by the ALCOR volunteers. Benny Ray said at the time, "We have this red dye that they swish around in their mouths after they brush, and wherever they miss a place, the red dye stays and tells on them. The one who does the best job wins a tube of toothpaste."

The program also helped to identify those who were not receiving care that was already available. Benny Ray told the South Bend Review's Bob Cooper, in 1970, "One student found a lady who had been turned down for public assistance, but she had later been examined by two Lexington doctors and had been given total disability by them. She didn't know she could go back to the public assistance people and make another application on the basis of this new information. We helped her do that." The Floyd County Times also reported that, "Medical students from the University of Kentucky have helped, too, by doing blood tests and urine tests, to complement the height, weight and eye examinations given by the nurses. ALCOR students win the confidence of the people in these isolated areas, and this provides an entry for local professional people to give more help. This system paved the way for home visits in which the student nurses found such things as a child with polio who had never been treated by a physician, a person with hepatitis, who had not seen a doctor. The nurses made referrals of the polio case and helped organize gamma globulin injections in the area where the hepatitis was found."

ALCOR was a summer program, but the volunteers did not allow that to limit the attention they gave to those they served. Benny Ray reported, "In the fall, these students go back to the hollows and visit the families with whom they lived, and the people with whom they worked. They see that Johnny is doing well in reading. That everybody is back in school. They find ways to help during the winter months."

What made ALCOR different from so many summer programs available for students to "give back" was that ALCOR was focused on bringing Appalachian students together with Appalachian people. As so many Appalachians were suspicious of outsiders, they were especially suspicious of outsiders who were trying to change their ways. This only recalled the years of outsiders coming from the North to "civilize" the Scotch-Irish settlers. ALCOR volunteers had grown up in hollows much like those they were serving through the program. They weren't outsiders, they were insiders returning with new information. This made all the difference.

The South Bend Tribune's Bob Cooper wrote, "Gary Johnson is 18 years old, a sophomore this fall in college, but he's an expert at knowing what children in remote Appalachian hollows like this one want and need. He was raised here." Cooper also wrote that, "locally reared college students establish rapport with residents of an area as a prelude to more conventional anti-poverty programs... the bait is recreation." Cooper observed that at the ALCOR community center, children could be seen "playing with toys their parents could never afford, receiving encouragement in health practices, being encouraged to demonstrate creativity in drawing." Benny Ray told Cooper, "It's not our idea to teach people to hook rugs, although that's a pretty good hobby. But while they're all there, it's a perfect opportunity to discuss child care, diets, and things like that."

Although they had a medicinal agenda, the ALCOR program and volunteers were focused on recognizing community needs and providing solutions. The Floyd County Times recounts one instance in which an ALCOR team rehabilitated a slate mountain, which is a mountain made of coal removal waste. Gary Johnson tells Cooper, "The county loaned us a grader for three days and we smoothed out the slate pile, then scraped dirt off the mountain, to cover it with about six inches." At the end of seven weeks, the ALCOR team transformed the coal industry's wasteland into a playground with swings, a merry-go-round, park benches, and barbecue grills. Inside, Cooper again quotes the young ALCOR volunteer, Gary Johnson, who said of the program's effects, "When these kids go to school, there are seven grades taught in this one building—and just two teachers. You can guess how much personal attention they get... When they go home, maybe there are seven or eight other children in the house, so you can judge how much personal attention they're going to get there. So you give a kid something to remember, that somebody cares about him, and when he grows up, he's not going to forget it."

The Floyd County Times reported that the ACLOR students, "walk miles beyond the road ends to get to the far hollows and the higher hills where their own people not only welcome their fresh influence but work with them toward a better life for young and old. In a few locations they have met misunderstandings from people who have been exploited and even misled by 'up lifters' from beyond the mountains." The Times quotes Charles Clark, Floyd County superintendent of schools, who said, "Ben Bailey is doing a grand job with ALOR students. Folks should not mix them up with outsiders who come in here to foist their own ideas on our people."

The Floyd County Times reported that, "The program has private and public funds, including $109,000 from the Bruner Foundation, $1,000 from Reader's Digest, $52,000 from the Appalachian Regional Commission for the nursing component, and $100,000 from the four colleges involved. Also, a pharmaceutical company donated $10,000 worth of toothbrushes, toothpaste, red dye, shampoo and other supplies." Benny Ray was an impassioned advocate for his cause, and considered it a worthy investment: "These students wash and set the little girls hair, then let them make appointments like they would with a hairdresser. They teach them cleanliness by example and by lesson. They bring the parents into it, too, by visiting them at home or talking to them at the centers about nutrition, hygiene, and such things."

One of the nurses, Miss Howell, also reported helping the children write and produce plays for their parents: "One was about a little girl who was dying of malnutrition because she was eating the wrong kinds of foods. It was kind of heavy drama, but it was good propaganda, and the parents enjoyed it." She also recalled, "When I came here, three- fourths of the children were not eating breakfast, and most of them wouldn't eat vegetables at home, even though their mothers fixed them...I think we've got that problem solved this summer."

Guy L. Smith, of Letcher County's The Mountain Eagle called ALCOR's work, "a significant step in the service of mankind." The article paints a vivid picture of the scene, where "Outhouses dot the countryside, causing pollution in the spring-fed creeks when rains flood them. Running water is also seldom seen and each of the homes is equipped with a backyard well, usually fettered out of the ground with a shovel. After a long, dusty hike from where the car had to stop, the one-room cinder block school-house-community-center comes into view. Shirtless and shoeless youngsters dart back and forth in the carefree play while Connie, the pretty 21-year-old student nurse, patiently counsels a little boy against drinking the water in the polluted creek that quietly flows by the school house."

Smith noted that another valuable part of ALCOR's work, which was to collect data about the region's often reclusive citizens: "They have gathered valuable data in their untiring work, as well as being extremely helpful to the residents. The data will help them, and others, determine the most severe problems and assist in setting up priorities for work in the hollows...Mental retardation, infant deaths, and communicable diseases are widespread.

"School dropout rates are high, and amongst the most serious problems in regard to education are lack of parents' understanding of educational needs, withdrawal characteristics, low self-esteem, non- competitiveness, and disregard for the future."

Smith reported that, "One of the most successful programs under ALCOR was the introduction of fresh fruit in the children's diet every day when they came to the schoolhouse to learn and play with Connie." One volunteer noted that she inspired attendance at the camp by beating all of the children at sports. "If I can beat them, then they have to come back and play with me till they beat me," she said. In addition to the benefit of increased positive attention from adults, the nutritional benefits of the program alone were often enough to create dramatic change in the children who participated. Smith wrote that, "Often times a listless child has become cheerful and alert when he has had a nutritious snack. In striking cases, parents actually thought their child was unable to talk, until a nutritional diet and activity changed the whole life of the child."

In 1970, the ALCOR program was featured in a study entitled, "The Myth of Rural Non-Involvement," by Abraham W. Baily and Thomas R. Sawyer of California State College. This study noted that, "Grady, and Benny Bailey, who is the vice president for operations of ALCOR, both were raised in the immediate area and have worked with ALCOR since its earliest days. They serve as prime examples of indigenous people who have provided the continuity of energy, creativity, and aspirations that have brought ALCOR to the point where it is now reaching 14,000 to 16,000 people every year. Today ALCOR is generally recognized as a spectacularly successful example of what can happen when educational, social, and medical resources are combined with student energy and enthusiasm. ACLOR President Raymond LeRoux referred to Benny and Grady as living examples of how 'lil ole holler kids' can become successful."

This study also featured another notable story about ALCOR's work: "Union College students answered the emergency needs of the Pentecostal Children's Home south of Barbourville, Ky., the only full- service children's home in a county of 25,000. The state had notified the institution that it no longer could be licensed for operation unless a case history was developed on each of the 39 children in the home. The children ranged in age from four to twenty, and funds were not available to hire full- time social workers to establish these records, so student volunteers began compiling the case histories. The size of the student volunteer force quickly grew to 50, many of whom as they completed the records, also became involved in non-administrative aspects of the home's operation, such as leading recreation programs and fixing broken bicycles."

In 1971, Business Week reported on the success of ALCOR, which they noted was the first program of its kind to succeed in Appalachia. The article quotes Ben Slone, a 76- year old resident of Slone's Fork, who said that the ALCOR students were "the finest people I've ever met." The article also noted that "the most important person behind ALCOR—and possibly the best role model in Appalachia— was Benny Ray Bailey," who they also noted was just in his early twenties at this time. This article also reported that Grady and Benny were considering establishing a full-time clinic.

Grady Stumbo and Benny Ray Bailey proved to be an exceptional team. Grady was in charge of the medical aspects of the program; for example, the nursing students would do screening and go around the community educating about basic healthcare. At the end of each summer, Benny Ray and Grady debriefed every ALCOR student. They asked, "What did you see and would you come to Appalachia for part or all of your professional life?" They almost always said, "Yes," that they would come back. They would ask the students, "What have you seen that's working?" And the students said, "Nothing." They'd ask, "What would you like to see?" And the student volunteers routinely replied, "A clinical facility, with a lab, x-ray, etc., run by an organization governed by the community, a community organization, where professionals worked for a salary and in a team, with registered nurses and dentists and pharmacists."

Nothing like that existed, so Benny Ray and Grady set out to create it.

That ALCOR was an outstanding success has been well documented. A tremendous amount of the credit for this belongs to those on each individual college campus who supported and directed the program. Local colleges gave a community credibility to the program, which was lacking from other "brought on" programs in the anti-poverty programs of the federal and state government.

The Presidents of the local colleges were Will Hayes at Alice Lloyd College, the spiritual leader of ALCOR; George Luster, at Southeast Community College, who spent countless hours working for ALCOR without pay; Troy Eslinger at Less Junior College, who always offered invaluable advice; Jim Boswell at Cumberland College, who was more committed to assisting the young people of Appalachia than anyone in the program; Marvin Jolly the energetic and outspoken President of Hazard Community College; and Mahlon Miller at Union College, who traveled with Benny Ray to call on foundations and corporations to elicit support. These Presidents of local colleges gave unselfishly of their time and resources to assist their students in gaining valuable community services, experience, and residents of the communities they served unparalleled summer educational enrichment programs.

Another key person in ALCOR was Raymond K. LeRoux. Ray came to ALCOR as President in December, 1970. Ray was an excellent fundraiser, and was a great asset in bringing financial stability to ALCOR. He remained with ALCOR for one year. The campus directors and assistant directors at the participating colleges worked tirelessly to support the students and give them legitimacy in their communities. Shannon Bailey, Deano Johnson at Alice Lloyd College, Mike Smathers at Lees Junior College, Bruce Ayers, Murris Wilder, and Reecie Stagnolia at Southeast Community College, Julian Mosley and Laura Mosley at Union College, Ralph Rhoden and Richard Brashear at Cumberland College, John Brown and Dee Davis at Hazard Community College, were a big part of the success of ALCOR. At the end of the program in the early 1980's, ALCOR was one of the longest running, if not the longest running, student community service program in America.

CHAPTER FOUR

A DIFFERENT KIND OF UNION CARD

In the winter of 1970, Benny Ray attended Ohio University for one quarter to begin work on his doctorate. Bill Hughes had attended OU and encouraged Benny Ray to begin his work at this school. At this time, Benny Ray was convinced that he would spend the rest of his life in positions in higher education, and he knew that to advance in the field of higher education, he would need a "union card," i.e. a Ph.D.

The doctoral program at Ohio University required 128 hours of college course work beyond the bachelor's degree; passing an advanced writing examination; completion of two competences, one of which had to be a foreign language; completion of the comprehensive exam at the end of the class work; and writing a dissertation acceptable to the committee advising the Ph.D. candidate. Not an easy road. That's why in the 1970s, the average age of a person completing the Ph.D. was 42 while the average age of a person completing the M.D. was 28.

After the winter quarter at OU, Benny Ray returned to Pippa Passes to direct the ALCOR program. Before leaving OU, he had talked to his doctoral committee about allowing him to take courses relating to a specific state (e.g., school law, school curriculum, and school finance) at a Kentucky college. The committee agreed.

In the 1970-1971 school year, Benny Ray drove the 100 miles from Alice Lloyd College to Morehead State University to take evening courses which he then transferred to Ohio University. These courses were accepted at Ohio University into his doctoral program.

Also during the 1970-1971 school year, Benny Ray was directing the ALCOR program and serving as Director of Admissions at Alice Lloyd College. However, one of the requirements of the doctoral program at Ohio University was three successive quarters of residency on the campus in Athens, Ohio. So, in 1971, Benny Ray informed the ALCOR Board of Directors that he would resign from the program after the summer of 1971 to complete his Ph.D. program at Ohio University.

At their annual meeting in December, 1971, the ALCOR Board of Directors hired Raymond K. LeRoux to replace Benny Ray as the CEO of ALCOR. Ray was very skilled at developing funds and he and Benny Ray set out in the winter of 1971 to raise the needed funding for the ALCOR program.

While the two men traveled the nation in search of funds, they concentrated their work in the New York City metropolitan area. The results were astounding; grants from the Rockefeller Foundation ($100,000), the Fannie E. Rippel Foundation ($70,000), the W.K. Kellogg Foundation ($233,000), IBM ($30,000), the Western Electric Fund ($5,000), and funding from a class action suit from the Kentucky Attorney General's

Office ($500,000), along with other grants, made over $1 million available for the ALCOR program. Working with Ray LeRoux, developing private foundation and corporate grants, would prove invaluable to Benny Ray later as he developed grants to build a medical clinic.

In the fall of 1971, Business Week did an article about ALCOR called "Appalachia Gets a Program It Trusts." The article was read by Mr. John D. Rockefeller III. Mr. Rockefeller called Benny Ray and invited him to a conference of young leaders that his foundation, the JDR III Youth Fund, was hosting in Maryland. Mr. Rockefeller's staff, who were conducting the conference, were Dick Barrett and Jack Haar. Jack Haar later became Vice President of ABC News. These two men were a great help to Benny Ray later as he sought funding for a medical clinic in Appalachia.

Benny Ray's roommate at the conference was a fellow named John Whitehead. John's father had developed a company called Technicon that made blood analysis machinery. This connection proved very helpful as plans for the medical clinic in Appalachia took shape in later years.

In the fall of 1971, Benny Ray returned to Ohio University to complete the course work for his doctorate. He also continued to work for ALCOR and traveled with the ALCOR Board members to call on foundations and corporations throughout America. He also continued to serve on various national committees as a result of his contacts with the Rockefeller group.

In the spring quarter of 1972, Benny Ray completed the course work for his doctorate. He had also passed the advanced writing test, challenged the GRE Foreign Language Test in German (his undergraduate minor was German), and passed the comprehensive examinations. He was ready to begin work on establishing the medical clinic in Appalachia. During the next few years, Benny Ray forgot about his doctoral work as he developed the funding and the administrative plans for the medical clinic. In 1972, Grady Stumbo completed his M.D. and returned to east Kentucky; in 1972, Benny Ray completed his course work for the doctorate and returned to east Kentucky. Together, they set about building the first medical clinic facility in the small Kentucky county of Knott. However, Benny Ray also had some unfinished business in completing his doctoral program, namely writing and getting approval of a doctoral dissertation.

One of the national committees Benny Ray served on was a committee formed by the United States Department of Education called "Education Renewal for the 1970's." This committee met throughout America and included such notables as Margaret Mead, Amatai Etzeoni, and futurist Bob Theobald. One of the committee members was Sam Goldwyn.

Sam Goldyn and Benny Ray became friends as they served on this committee. One evening, at dinner in Minneapolis, Sam questioned Benny Ray for quite some time about the School of Education at Ohio University. Benny Ray told Sam he really enjoyed his time there and had a very high opinion of the School of Education at OU.

Finally, Benny Ray asked Sam, "Why are you so interested in the School of Education at OU?"

Sam replied, "They offered me the position of Dean of the School of Education and, after talking with you, I think I will accept."

At this point, Benny Ray had completed all the requirements for the Ph.D. except the dissertation. In higher education circles this is referred to as "ABD" or "all but dissertation."

Beginning in 1973, Dr. Max Evans, Director of the Educational Administration Department at Ohio University, began to call Benny Ray and encourage him to complete his dissertation. Sam Goldwyn had also called and encouraged Benny Ray.

In 1974, Benny Ray presented a proposal to his doctoral committee for a dissertation entitled "A Case Study of the First Year of Development of East Kentucky Health Services Center, Inc." The committee accepted the proposal and he began work on the dissertation. One interesting note: in 1990, then State Senator Benny Ray Bailey successfully passed the "Health Care Reform Act of 1990," which included much of his dissertation, making Benny Ray's dissertation one of the very few doctoral dissertations in the history of American higher education to be written into state law.

In 1975, one and one half years after he started, Benny Ray defended his dissertation successfully and was granted the Ph.D. at the 1975 commencement at Ohio University. The dissertation was completed while Benny Ray was developing the plans and the funding for the medical clinic as well as recruiting the personnel to operate the first clinical facility in the history of Knott County.

CHAPTER FIVE

BEGINNING THE CLINIC

Their time at Alice Lloyd College had instilled a strong desire to work with their native Appalachian community in both Dr. Grady Stumbo and Benny Ray Bailey. Even while they were still attending school there, the two began to dream of building a center for the community that would provide them with the basic medical care they so often lacked. Stumbo would later say that during his time at Alice Lloyd College, he and Bailey "sorta got infected with the concept that one is supposed to do more for mankind than make money." Working with the ALCOR program gave both men a practical framework for these dreams. Through ALCOR, they gained hands-on experience with what delivering medical care to the rural hill towns would entail. They saw how it could both provide an important service to the community and serve as a way to keep Kentucky's brightest minds anchored to their home, giving them a reason to stick around instead of going to other cities for work, as had so long been the trend.

It can be hard for someone who grew up outside of Appalachia to understand how isolated the people in the region truly were in the 1970s. Located near the Virginia border in the heart of

Appalachia, Knott County (and its neighboring regions) had been completely dominated by the coal industry for decades, but no one had bothered to install the infrastructure that would ensure the miners had basic necessities, like clean water and nutritious food. In part, this was because of the challenge presented by the scattered population. Most residents lived in tiny mining towns spread through the hollows. At the time Bailey and Stumbo started their clinic outside of Hindman, it had a population of only 808 people—and that as the county seat. The median per capita income for Knott County in 1970, meanwhile, was only $1,152 (the national median per capita income at this time was $6,186).

When Stumbo bought the land that would become the East Kentucky Health Services Center, the area had two doctors to tend to the 16,000 people living in Knott County. Getting an x-ray meant traveling to the hospital at Hazard; other lab work could mean going as far as the University of Kentucky. There were no local clinics and patients often had to wait several hours to get care, if they could get care at all— with no call centers, needing medical attention outside of the office's hours meant driving as much as 40 miles to reach the nearest hospital. Only one doctor in the county could deliver babies and he could only do it at his office, meaning many women used midwives for delivery. Dental care in the region was virtually non-existent.

In the course of their work with ALCOR, Bailey and Stumbo spoke with the nursing, health science, and other student volunteers who'd spent time in the summer program, finding out what ideas they had about setting up a plan for year-round health care in the Knott County region. By 1971, they had an impressive sample size; the program had grown to include 1,500 health science students from 78 different medical schools, including many students from the eastern Kentucky area. Bailey and Stumbo were quickly able to identify the region's lack of adequate medical facilities as the main reason physicians wouldn't come to work in Knott County. The debriefings done with the student volunteers who worked with ALCOR revealed that most of them (around 80%) would consider returning to the region to keep working in the future, but the overwhelming majority (around 98%) wouldn't want to work under the existing conditions. Nearly all of them called for a clinical facility, complete with labs and x-ray equipment, which would let them practice comprehensive medicine.

It became clear that if they wanted to entice doctors and nurses to practice medicine in the region long-term, a well-equipped facility would be an absolute necessity, especially since one of the clinic's long-term goals was to sell graduate students on service in Appalachia. Stumbo wanted medical professionals to see that, in coming to the region to work, "they don't have to sacrifice their professional ability." On the graduate students, he said, "We think a lot of them are looking for a challenge and we think there is a certain percentage of young professionals who will buy it." These certainties, paired with the information and suggestions they'd received from the ALCOR participants, influenced the construction and operation of the clinic in Knott County.

Their work with ALCOR was not the only thing Stumbo and Bailey did to lay the groundwork for their new clinic before they bought the land in 1972. In the fall of 1971, the pair met with Ray LeRoux, at that time the director of the ALCOR program. Together, they signed the incorporation papers that officially created the East Kentucky Health Services Center. Bailey was named the chairman of the corporation and would handle the administrative aspects; Stumbo was the president and medical director. The center would exist only on paper for the next eight months while Stumbo finished his medical schooling and Bailey completed the coursework for his Ph.D., but the signing of the papers was an important step in making the center real. It served as a legal verification that they were coming back to Knott County and were prepared to stay for the long haul.

In June of 1972, Benny Ray had completed his doctoral coursework through Ohio University. Though it would take him three more years to complete his dissertation, he could do that while continuing his work in eastern Kentucky. Stumbo finished with his schooling and returned to Knott County, as well. Both men were ready to apply their education and experience to their long-time dream.

In the spring of 1972, Grady Stumbo took a corporate bond resolution he'd written himself to a bank in Hindman and obtained a loan for $10,000 to purchase the clinic site. Benny Ray recounts the day Stumbo called him to say he'd borrowed the money, "And by the way you borrowed it, too." Later reports made on the clinic once it was open and thriving described how they transformed "$53 and a dream" into a million- dollar facility. Most people would be terrified of taking on such a massive endeavor with no definite funding in place, but as Stumbo would later say, "We knew we'd do it even if we had to have the clinic in a tent." There had been many young sons of Appalachia who'd opened private practices elsewhere in the country after they got out of medical school, with plans to save up money then move home and open a clinic. But Bailey had noticed how those plans never seemed to materialize, saying, "But if you do that, you work a year and then you've got a car to pay for; then after another year or two you've got kids and a house and you never get around to doing it."

Bailey and Stumbo were not about to risk having this happen to them—and they weren't completely without financial means. Stumbo had started working at Our Lady of the Way hospital in the town of Martin in nearby Floyd County (about a 30--minute drive from the future site of the clinic). Between this income and the loan from the bank in Hindman, they were able to purchase some bottom land at the mouth of Troublesome Creek, what Bailey described as "a swamp full of horseweeds" a few miles outside the Knott County town of Hindman. Bailey set about the task of finding more funding for the project while Stumbo continued to work at Our Lady of the Way to raise capital of his own.

One reason the ALCOR program under Bailey's direction had been so successful was because he understood the Appalachian mindset. He took pride in his hillbilly heritage and understood the pride the mountain folk had in themselves. People living in the region didn't want to be given handouts, or to have their way of life questioned by outsiders in exchange for getting services they needed. Because Stumbo was a native son of the region, people knew he understood this about them and trusted him to act in their best interest, not to exploit or mislead them as outsiders had in the past. Paul Stark, with whom Stumbo worked at Our Lady of the Way, said that people felt positively inclined toward Grady, and that "there's pride too, that he's not from a family doctors usually come from. His father was a miner. And they're grateful he came back because most don't." Dr. Stumbo shared this sentiment of familiarity and pride.

When he spoke on this topic to <u>Modern Medicine</u> in 1975, he said, "They're my people. It's like when I went to medical school. At U.K., the hillbillies are considered the red-necks...I'd always say, 'Well I'm a hillbilly.' And they'd say, 'Well, we're not talkin' about you. You're different.' Hell, I ain't no different, man! And you think I'm gonna sit here and let you talk about my people and then you're gonna like me? You talk about hillbillies in front of me and I'm gonna run all over you. And this is the kind of thing Alice Lloyd taught me: 'Remember where you came from. 'Because it'll catch up with you.'"

Understanding the people and the region altered the way the East Kentucky Health Services

Center (called the EKHSC, for short) was to be designed and staffed. As with the ALCOR program, they planned to use a combination of outsiders and "home folk," people who were from other hollows in east Kentucky if they weren't necessarily from Knott County. The first two registered nurses to sign on with the clinic had worked in the region before through the ALCOR program, meaning that—though they were technically outsiders, one from Georgia and one from Minnesota—they knew the area and, more importantly, the people. A second physician, Dr. Roger Akers, who also hailed from McDowell (the same town as the two clinic founders), which was located in the next county over, joined the staff in 1973.

The goal of the EKHSC was to provide primary care to families in the region (at a cost they could afford) while still being a self- sustaining entity that wouldn't rely on federal funding. To do this required a radical re- thinking of how health care was provided. Drawing off of the strong family bonds inherent to hill people, the clinic sent health advocates to the patients' homes and taught their families how to help them handle many aspects of the treatment, from checking blood pressure to administering medicine. By educating members of the community on how to maintain their own health—and giving regular screenings to catch problems in early stages, when they're more easily treatable—the clinic could do more for the overall health of the community with fewer on-staff physicians. This allowed the center to bring the small communities of the hills the same comprehensive health care offered to residents of bigger cities.

Construction on the clinic began in November of 1972. They prepared the land themselves, borrowing a bulldozer from Dr. Stumbo's stepfather to clear out the weeds and set up trailers. By New Year's Day, 1973, the clinic was seeing its first patients and had more professionals—including a dentist and a paramedic—set to join the staff in the coming year. They'd also negotiated a contract with Our Lady of the Way hospital (where Stumbo worked) that let them send patients along who required hospitalization. They might have started it as a "nickel and dime" operation, but they'd started something groundbreaking, and planned to be entirely self-sufficient within three years.

To start it all off, of course, they'd need more than the $53 they came back to Knott County with. Bailey's work fundraising for ALCOR had given him some background in asking foundations for funding and some experience with where to look, but finding financing was still difficult. As Bailey said, "When you talk like we do, most people think of the typical hillbilly, the uneducated person they show on TV. They had no guarantee that we would not run away with the money."

Still, Benny Ray Bailey was a born salesman, and he had an excellent idea to sell with the clinic he and Stumbo planned to build. He started his interactions with philanthropists by knocking them out with enthusiasm. Once he had their interest, he would show them the solid plans they'd built about how to get the clinic off the ground. Once they'd purchased the land, Bailey went to New York to meet face to face with potential investors. He talked to private foundations, to medical equipment manufacturers—pretty much to anyone with money who would listen.

This is not to say that it worked right away. There were a few tense months after the land was purchased in July until the first of the donations began to come in. Bailey describes them taking the phone off the hook, sometimes for a few days at a time, to avoid the calls from creditors. But Bailey's hard work—and both partners' faith—paid off. Bailey made contact with the JDR III Foundation while he was in New York. Bailey recalls, "They called and asked me to come to a conference and spend a couple of weeks with them." He attended the Conference Board's dinner and gave a speech about the clinic. It was a great success; they'd found a significant source of funding, and the John D. Rockefeller Third Task Force on Youth saved their project from failing before it could truly begin. By August 1972 they had enough to begin construction on the clinic, and by December 31, when they were set to open their doors, they had raised over $150,000 in private funds—and this in just the six months since they bought the land.

The matter of getting funding for the clinic was somewhat complicated by the fact that neither Bailey nor Stumbo wanted to make use of any federal funding. There was a strong distrust for programs brought in by the federal government among the people of the hollows due to bad experiences in the past. Federal money did still come into the area, but it mostly went to larger towns, like Hazard and Prestonsburg, and never seemed to funnel down to the hollows. Bailey understood and shared this "innate mountain suspicion of the feds," but it wasn't simply an ideological disparity that kept them from pursuing federal funds. The process for gaining funds involved extensive, time-consuming paperwork and research. To get $100,000 in funds from the government, the pair estimated they'd need to spend around $20,000 to conduct the surveys and needed studies that would justify it—money they certainly didn't have to waste.

Government funding meant "too many strings attached, too much lethargy setting in," as Grady Stumbo would later say. By obtaining only private funding, they could run their clinic their way, and get it running more quickly, without letting bureaucrats have even indirect control over the project.

Even without taking any government funds, however, Bailey continued to find new sources of funding for the clinic, eventually getting over $625,000 in donations from private foundations. The largest portion of this came from the Robert Wood Johnson Foundation, which Bailey had read about in the paper while he was in New York. After meeting with Bailey and going over his proposal, they donated $400,000 to the budding clinic (in a 1975 report, the foundation called the East Kentucky Health Services Center the "crowning jewel" of their first three years). The center also got major contributions from the Kresge Foundation, the Ripple Foundation, and the Beth-Elkhorn Corporation—nearly 20 private foundations in total, many of whom gave decreasing support over a three- year period.

Some foundations that didn't give monetary donations to the clinic still helped them to get off of the ground by donating laboratory or medical equipment. In many instances, this meant the Knott County clinic was able to get equipment even more advanced than what was available at the big hospitals elsewhere in the state. Bailey's roommate at the JDR III Foundation conference was a young man named John Whitehead. His father had founded Technicon and gave the clinic blood analysis machinery worth between $150,000 and $200,000. "We had the only equipment that did that," Bailey said, "so the credibility went to the top of the class really quick."

During the early months of setting up the clinic, the duo also sought the advice of some mentors and experts in the fields of both medicine and business. Dr. Donald Madison from the University of North Carolina School of Medicine and Dr. William Linville, chairman of the medical economics department at Stanford University, both helped to analyze the clinic's operations as it started treating customers and came up with economic solutions for the clinic moving forward. By their estimates, it would be possible for the clinic to become self- sustaining in 36-48 months. Stumbo and Bailey set out to achieve that goal.

Health screenings that had been done by volunteers from the ALCOR program revealed some serious problems that had long gone untreated in the hollow population. The region had long been underserved by medical professionals and this left the clinic with a lot of work to do and not many resources to do it, but they'd anticipated these challenges when they started. The screenings from ALCOR only helped to better prepare them for the hard work ahead.

Bringing medical care to rural Appalachia was a task with unique challenges. Even though both Bailey and Stumbo were "native sons," they knew they'd face some initial resistance until they earned the local trust. Most of the medical students who'd be doing the community outreach aspect of the clinic's work were outsiders; until the center built its reputation, the locals had no reason to trust them. To combat this, they made a point of including college students who'd been born in the area in each examination team that went out to make home visits, ensuring there would always be someone in the group that understood the hillbilly way of life. Dr. Stumbo made sure all the staff understood that they'd be a bit suspect in their patients' eyes at first, and that it was the product of past bad experiences, nothing personal. It didn't take long for Knott County's residents to realize the East Kentucky clinic's people were really there to help; acceptance of the nurses and medical students soon reached nearly 100 percent.

From a medical perspective, the local economic climate presented its own challenges. Since many of the men worked in the coal mine, lung disease was common. The high poverty rate meant many children were chronically undernourished, while a lifetime of poor diet for the adults led to issues with obesity, hypertension, and cardiovascular disease. Because there had never been a clinic in the area before, a lot of the emphasis in the first few years of operation was on education— teaching families what a well-balanced diet looked like, for example, or instructing the children on good dental hygiene, similar missions to what ALCOR had accomplished but with the medical facilities and equipment to take it to the next step. As soon as the clinic opened in 1972, they used money from the Clark Foundation to set up four student health teams. Setting up a system for them to communicate over the phone, Stumbo had the student health teams establish public health screening at the elementary school, along with private screening in visits to patients' homes. These exams were more extensive than your traditional physical and were designed specifically to address the region's challenges. It included dental exams, vision tests, and even blood and urine samples along with the typical blood pressure and heartbeat measurements. People who were screened received a letter shortly after either giving them a clean bill of health or telling them they should come to the clinic to see a doctor. Many times these screenings would catch conditions the sufferer wasn't even aware of, letting the clinic's staff start treatment before the ailment could become serious.

This preventative approach to medicine was the underlying principle behind the clinic's operation. Dr. Stumbo described medical care "like a cliff. When you're healthy, you're on top of the cliff, but then you fall off and you're sick." The old approach to primary care— especially in rural areas—was just to pick the person up and put them back at the top of the cliff, without making sure they wouldn't fall off again. At the Knott County clinic, the idea was "to build a fence around that cliff, one post at a time, and the outreach program of medical screening is that fence." During their first year, the clinic was able to screen over 20% of the county's population, and made it possible for every child in the county who entered first grade in August of that year to have a complete physical for the first time in many years.

Though the screenings and preventative care were the underlying goal of the clinic's early years, they also treated the community's illnesses and injuries, mostly on an outpatient rather than an overnight basis. By November of 1973, the clinic had a daily case load of around 85 patients per day—this with only two physicians on staff. To effectively treat all the patients, the clinic utilized what they called "physician extenders," which included the registered nurses, physician's assistants, lab technicians, and medical students who were on the staff. The physician extenders worked in five-man teams and handled the routine care. The physicians would personally review all the records to stay on top of everything going on in the clinic, but were able to give their attention where it was needed most without becoming overworked, as the region's other doctors had been.

The clinic also used the strong family ties so prevalent in the Appalachian people to extend their care into the residents' homes and everyday lives. "Don't ever ask a family member to leave the room in my presence," Dr. Stumbo said in one interview, "I've got nothing to hide and everyone benefits from the relationship... once you begin to break off the mysticism of medicine, common people find it extremely exciting." When sickness was found, they treated it as a family matter. They made arrangements for the residents to get the medical equipment they needed for complete home care and paired this equipment with education. Family members were instructed in the routine care and treatment of the ailment— and what signs to look for that meant it was time to take the patient back to the clinic. Dr. Stumbo described one patient success story about a miner with chronic lung disease who'd been hospitalized repeatedly, around once a month before the Knott County clinic opened. Thanks to the patient teaching program through the new clinic, the man was able to avoid hospitalization for nearly a year. When the families did come into the clinic—whether it was for routine care or a serious ailment— they aimed to make it a one-stop process for the entire family whenever possible. Mom, dad, kids, and extended family could come in at the same time and each get a check-up—and all be in the loop about each other's health.

Over half of the patients who used the clinics had some kind of health insurance, either through the government in the form of Medicare and Medicaid or a program from the United Mine Workers Union. The uninsured residents presented a different challenge. About 35% of the local population was indigent and couldn't afford regular medical care— but the Appalachian pride prevented Bailey and Stumbo from simply giving the services away for free. The mountain people were embarrassed by hand- outs; if the service was free, many of them would stay home and suffer, even when they were sick, rather than seek out the clinic. Their solution to this problem was to set up a sliding payment scale based on income and need. "Nobody gets it free," Dr. Stumbo said in an interview, "Of course, you can't get blood out of a turnip, so we let them pay what they can...Even if they only pay 50 cents, it makes them feel that they've share in the cost." By their second year of operation, the clinic was giving out around $4,000 in patient care discounts each month on a subjective system that allowed any of the providers to discount the services when they saw the need.

The East Kentucky Health Services Center still had plans to become self-sufficient within three years, and patient fees were a large part of that plan. For those with insurance (and the others who could afford to pay) the EKHSC calculated the fees for services at around 10% above cost, with the charges determined by a sophisticated computer system that had been programmed by a Ph.D. candidate from Stanford University, Mike Higgins, who spent eight months at the clinic as part of his Stanford education program. Actually, in 1975, the clinic, through the generosity of the Fannie E. Rippel Foundation, had bought the first personal computer (PC), an IBM System 32, and, after the programming by Mike Higgins, became the first primary care center in Kentucky, and quite possibly the nation, to computerize its business and medical operation. The computer programs were given to other primary care centers at no cost to them. As Bailey said in a 1975 interview with <u>Modern Medicine</u>, "You can't build a clinic in the ghetto and you can't build a clinic in Knott County and serve only poor people.

Because the one common denominator of poor people the world over is that they ain't got no money! They can't pay! For us to survive here and provide about $4,000 a month in discount services, we have to get money from people who have it." He went on to say, "People come here for health services. All people. It's not a poor people's clinic; it's not a rich people's clinic. It's a people's clinic."

Bailey and Stumbo knew that, by using their sophisticated system, they could increase their earnings as a clinic—and as employees of it—if they didn't give out such hefty discounts. But that wasn't the point of the clinic. From the beginning, they decided to pay their staff set salaries and turn any profits earned back into the clinic's operations. "If a doctor is going to keep all the profits," Bailey said, "he's out to make money and can't have the services we have here." Any savings they discovered through their computer system they passed on to the patients.

More importantly than the money and pricing, their system was able to identify trends in the patient population, determining the points and locations of greatest need so the clinic could continue to improve how it helped the community. Using this information (and about $65,000 in grant money) Bailey and Stumbo determined a mobile clinic was in order to help expand the capabilities of their community health advocates. They also discovered that nearly 40% of their patients were coming from a part of the county that was around 26 miles away; in response to learning that, the duo bought a plot of land near Kite in Knott County and began construction on a satellite clinic. The level of complexity and technological innovation utilized by the clinic to both streamline their daily operations and analyze the patterns of treatment in the region belied long-held misconceptions about the relative intelligence of hillbillies. As Bailey told The Courier- Journal & Times in 1976, "We're not just good old boys. Our computer is sophisticated and good old boys can't run it."

The radical new approach to primary care that Bailey and Stumbo brought to Appalachia quickly began to show results. The success stories were almost too numerous to track. One older woman had been suffering for some time from a central nervous system disease, but didn't even realize it until the screening team caught it; she was able to start receiving regular medical care. Another local family had chronic heart problems and hypertension, though they insisted they weren't eating any salt. Dr. Stumbo went to their home and found the drinking water from their spigots was overloaded with minerals—including sodium. He helped them fix the spigot, eliminating the cause of the issue rather than just treating the symptoms. As Bailey told the Courier-Journal in 1974, "We've had patients in here for such things as a broken arm and found out they have some disease they didn't even know about. That's the whole idea of our program."

By fall of 1974, the EKHSC was no longer the only game in town. The federally-funded June Buchanan Clinic opened in 1974 and saw over 100 patients on its first day of operation. The doctors who had previously operated offices in Knott County—Dr. Gene Watts and Dr. Denzil Barker—were moved into this new clinic, giving them the same access to good equipment the EKHSC had been enjoying for nearly two years.

Bailey and Stumbo had approached the June Buchanan Clinic when it was being developed, considering joining their team. In talking to the clinic's founders, though, they found the government funding put prohibitive demands on the operation. They wouldn't be able to run the kind of radical new care center they'd conceived of and ultimately decided to open their own clinic instead. Still, the opening of the June Buchanan Clinic further expanded the medical care available in the area, with their own full-time staff of over 30. A place that had no clinics just three short years' prior now had access to four doctors, two dentists, two pharmacists, about a dozen registered nurses and a complement of lab technicians. Both clinics offered 24/7 emergency room access, as well, putting an end to long drives down state route 80 to the Regional Hospital in Hazard for those Knott County residents who needed medical care at odd hours.

The EKHSC had been running for nearly two years when the June Buchanan Clinic opened. In that time, they'd generated nearly 12,000 patient charts, performed screening on over a third of the county's population, and were treating around 100 patients in the clinic each day. When Dr. Linville of Stanford University initially analyzed the clinic's operations, he anticipated they would be able to reach self-sustainability in 3-4 years. By the start of 1975, the clinic was completely free of debt— only 24 months after opening, and some two years ahead of schedule. The massive growth the clinic had seen in its first two years continued, both in terms of their staff numbers and the patients they saw.

The growth within the Knott County clinic, though, was not nearly as impressive as the changes Dr. Stumbo began to see in the state. When they broke ground on the clinic back in 1972 the state of Kentucky had no primary care centers; by 1976, there were seven—and soon to be eight, when the Kite clinic opened its doors later in the year. Stumbo described the state's primary care when he graduated medical school as "like a pregnant woman. Everyone knew it was coming but it hadn't gotten here yet." Now that it had arrived, it was exceeding even Bailey and Stumbo's hopes. The future of health care in Appalachia was bright; the Knott County clinic had a major role in shifting the emphasis from individual doctors to group and family care—and people outside of Kentucky were starting to take notice. Rural healthcare providers throughout the country started making that same shift. The educational and planning director for the Rural Health Associates, Paul Judkins, said in a 1976 interview with Group Practice that "physicians in the rural environment are learning to band together to maintain their sanity and collect the benefits of group practices."

Though neither Bailey nor Stumbo were particularly comfortable with the limelight now being shone on them, they were both proud of the work they'd already achieved and hopeful for what the future would bring. As Stumbo said in The Courier-Journal & Times in 1976, "In the beginning, we were trying to make the point that hard work and dedication could pay off. Now the time has come to emphasize that what we were saying is that this is a system, and it will work, and you have to modify it for your area." And it was working. Thanks to patient education, their well-equipped facility, and the mobile clinic's delivery of follow-up care, the Knott County clinic hospitalized less than 1% of their patients over their first few years of operation, and were getting closer to their goal of screening every member of the community. By the end of the 1979, they had over 18,000 patient charts in their system—a good 2,000 more than the population of the county.

Growth would continue to be the trend through the late '70s for the East Kentucky Health Services Center. Their staff expanded to include three physicians and two dentists. They were on strong enough footing by the start of 1978 that they were able to weather the storm when the United Mine Workers of America announced a strike, walking off their jobs on January 6. This suspended their health care program, one which had provided coverage for nearly 815,000 beneficiaries in the five-state soft coal region—in other words, the majority of the clinic's clientele. Even before the strike, changes to the insurance plan had pushed many miners away from seeking medical care, with deductibles rising to $500 or more. Many doctors who'd come to work in the region started getting second thoughts. Nearly 100 physicians abandoned Appalachia over the course of the extended strike, which would last through the summer. For the doctors at the Knott County clinics, though, medicine had never been about making money; for most of them, the striking miners were their people.

They broadly announced to local communities that their clinics would give the miners free health services until the strike ended and they were able to return to work. They recovered quickly from the dip in income prompted by the coal strike. By the start of 1979, the clinic had an annual budget of $550,000 and was seeing around 125 patients per day.

In Appalachian culture, people "look about their family," and that was just as true for those on the clinic's staff as it was in the patients they were treating. For both Bailey and Stumbo, their medical practice was a family affair. Benny Ray Bailey had met his wife, Nikki Rieck, when she worked as a student nurse with the ALCOR program as part of her studies.

Originally from Minnesota, she returned to her home state after the summer program ended— during the same span of time that Benny Ray spent at Ohio University's Athens campus finishing his doctoral coursework—but came back to Kentucky to help Bailey and Stumbo open their clinic. She was one of two nurses from the summer ALCOR program to be on the staff for opening day. Nikki and Benny Ray got married in 1973 and went on to have three sons (Benny Ray, Chet, and Steven) and one daughter, Rebekah, who died at birth. They lived together with Benny Ray's son Glenn from his first marriage. Nikki was a dedicated mother, not only leaving her work at the clinic to spend her time caring for the children but even getting a degree in elementary education so she could better help them through school.

She never lost her passion for health care, though; once the kids reached high school, she returned to the clinic as an administrator. Dr. Stumbo's wife, Jan, also worked as a nurse at the clinic. As Bailey's children got older, they would often help take care of the grounds keeping work on the land surrounding the clinic building.

Even the staff that hadn't come from the area couldn't help but be taken up in the family feel of the community. The people who came to work for the East Kentucky Health Services Center were dedicated to the region even if they hadn't been born there, and the staffers forged a familial connection over the course of their work. Though medical students would come and go and they would lose many physicians to private practice over the following years, the turnover rate among the staff at both Knott County clinics would stay incredibly low throughout their existence. This applied to both the physician extenders and the administration. Bailey recalls one office manager who stayed with the clinic for 37 years, a physician's assistant who stayed for 43 years, a receptionist who was there for 15— regardless of their discipline, those who came to work with the clinic soon found they were part of the family.

Bailey and Stumbo had said from the beginning that, while Appalachia was in their hearts and blood, this clinic was about more than bringing primary care to the Kentucky hollows. It was a model for rural healthcare that both believed could be applied successfully elsewhere in the country—and they weren't the only ones who felt this way. The Robert Wood Johnson Foundation was one of those that had given money to the project when it was first getting off the ground. About six months after they made their donation, Gus Lienhard (then the chairman of Johnson & Johnson as well as chair of the company's Board of Directors) came to visit Knott County along with David Rogers, President of the Robert Wood Johnson Foundation. They had to travel quite a ways to make the visit, driving 150 miles after flying in to a nearby airport, but their motivation for coming to see the clinic's work was worth the effort. They saw the potential of the system Bailey and Stumbo had established and wanted to make it work elsewhere in the country. Following their visit, they gave a $22 million grant to the University of North Carolina to help them establish similar programs across rural North America.

Given that the system was working so well in Knott County, the people who would be establishing these programs came to the EKHSC for training. The UNC program wasn't the only one to see the potential learning opportunity being presented in Knott County. Faculty members from other universities came to visit the clinic. Rob Sullivan, a professor at Duke, went through the screening program when he visited the school. He was charmed by the set-up, which used a lawn chair for a dentist's chair, and impressed by the service, saying afterwards, "That's the best dental exam I've had in my life."

The University of Kentucky medical school had used the clinic as a field teaching center nearly since its inception. Other students came in from colleges all across America as they had for the summer ALCOR program.

Though the emphasis remained on keeping health care within the community, they also wanted to bring in the best and brightest minds possible, and encouraged graduate and medical students from far and wide to come and work for a time in Knott County. Because the clinic was already on the radar of Dr. Linville at Stanford, that was one of the more distant schools that sent the most students to the program. One of the students who'd worked with Dr. Stumbo at the EKHSC was elected student body president after returning to his university. He'd been so impressed with the clinic's work that he pushed for Dr. Stumbo to give the commencement address in 1976—an honor that, in the past, had been reserved for university figures. Stumbo became the first non-faculty member to give a commencement speech at Stanford University.

In November of 1973, Associated Press writer Bob Cooper wrote a feature on the clinic that was picked up by newspapers across the United States. This brought a significant amount of national attention to the region and the clinic's work there. The American Medical Association's Committee on Health Care of the Poor invited Dr. Stumbo to talk with them about his project in March of 1974, just over a year after they'd officially opened their doors. Later, the American Bicentennial Committee brought in television crews and broadcast a 10-minute segment on the Knott County experiment, naming it a part of the national Bicentennial Program.

From May 31 to June 11, 1976, the United Nations Conference on Human Settlements took place in Vancouver, British Columbia. The goal of this conference was to identify solutions to the worldwide problems arising from "the rapid growth and change in the way people of the world live today and will live during the balance of the twentieth century." Each of the 140 nations that participated in this conference named demonstration projects from their homelands to share with the other participants, what they saw as their nation's best examples of innovative work "in such areas as housing and community development, land use, transportation, health, education, the environment and citizen involvement." The United States identified 200 official demonstration sites that they felt exemplified innovation in one or more of these areas. Since the conference was happening the same year as the Bicentennial celebration, the same organizations identified for the Horizons on Display Bicentennial program were used as demonstration sites for the U.N. Conference.

The East Kentucky Health Services Center was named for the Habitat portion of the demonstration, for exemplifying a novel approach to treating patients in the most rural areas of the country that could be applied across the world. The committee said it had been included because it "demonstrates [the] validity of building a health care program based upon sound management principles, without massive amounts of federal aid," a remarkable achievement wherever a health clinic was located. President Gerald Ford spoke highly of the center when reviewing the U.N. Conference sites, saying, "The East Kentucky Health Services Center is a prime example of the local initiative and private enterprise efforts that have made the United States the greatest country in the world over the past 200 years." Countless new visitors passed through the area following the announcement of the clinic as one of the demonstration sites. Foreign dignitaries with an interest in health sciences and rural medicine made visits to the demonstration sites on their way to the conference, adding international acclaim to the attention they'd already been receiving inside the United States. By 1979, the EKHSC had become the model for some 250 other health centers around the nation.

As the 1970s came to a close, the accolades for the clinic and Dr. Stumbo continued to pour in. On January 15, 1977, Stumbo was named one of America's Ten Outstanding Young Men by the U.S. Junior Chamber of Commerce. Nomination by a third party was necessary to be considered for the honor; in Dr. Stumbo's case, the people who'd nominated him had been his patients, exemplifying the pride and gratitude the region felt for the young doctor who'd come back home instead of seeking fortunes in the big cities. Always humble, Dr. Stumbo included Benny Ray Bailey in his success when the JayCees conferred the honor, telling reporters, "Anything I get I owe to him. We're separate people but very close." The following year, in December of 1978, both Stumbo and Bailey were honored with a Rockefeller Public Service Award.

As the scope and awareness of their Knott County experiment continued to expand beyond their familiar home hills, Bailey's perspective and aims grew with it. Several bills that would impact the way the East Kentucky Health Services Center—and all clinics statewide—could operate and staff their clinics were in the hopper for the Kentucky State Legislature when it met for its bi-annual session in 1976. Unfortunately, a lot of those bills failed because the various health organizations throughout the state were working as counter forces to each other. One legislative observer stated, "It was a circus, with one group sniping at the bill of another," regardless of the fact that many of the groups were going after the exact same end goals. As a result of the in-fighting, all of the bills failed; the various health centers would have to wait two more years, until the state legislature met again in 1978, to try again.

Benny Ray Bailey was one of those pushing for bills to pass during the 1976 legislative session, and was one of those frustrated by the confusion and failure. He figured if all the interested groups could share ideas and coordinate a strategy—rather than undercutting each other—they could help everyone gets the successful results they were looking for. In July of 1976, the Frontier Nursing Service sponsored a conference on primary care in Kentucky at the Mary Breckenridge Hospital in Hyden, Kentucky.

Bailey attended this conference, feeling out the idea of a comprehensive group that could work as a go-between with the legislative body and other government agencies. A month later, a smaller meeting was held in Hindman and the Kentucky Primary Care Association was officially incorporated. Benny Ray Bailey was named Chairman of the Board. It was a modest effort at the outset, run out of a drawer in Bailey's desk and with no budget or paid staff. Nonetheless, the KPCA soon grew to include over 200 individual members and 25 institutional members, all of whom were committed to working toward the same goals. Annual dues were set at $10 for individuals and between $25 and $100 for institutions, depending on the number of physicians at work in a given clinic.

The KPCA was designed as a forum for health professionals across disciplinary lines to share their experiences and resources, as well as to work as a collective force to implement changes and improvements in primary care delivery throughout Kentucky. The legislative aspect served as the first common interest problem for the Association to work on. The 1976 session wasn't the first time bills related to health care had come before the legislature and failed; the Kentucky legislature had been wrestling with similar bills since the start of the decade. The issue in question was a need for the state to legally define the status of mid-level practitioners, like physician assistants and nurse practitioners, and to adopt laws regulating the credentialing of health workers across disciplines.

Primary care centers needed these jobs to be officially defined at the state level if they wanted to be able to receive third-party reimbursement for the services they delivered. Since the state lacked certification laws, the clinics in the area were forced into inefficient staffing patterns—an especially damaging situation for the rural clinics, whose staff options and budgets were already tricky to coordinate.

The first annual meeting of the KPCA was held in October 1977 in Lexington, Kentucky. Over 200 people came to the city to attend the weekend conference, which was set up to address the first part of the organization's primary objective—to allow the various doctors, nurses, and other health professionals in the region to learn from each other and share experiences. Throughout the conference, those who were interested in designing a new set of legislation to put before the 1978 Kentucky legislature, one aimed at addressing the problem of certification for mid- level practitioners, were invited to meet at smaller sessions. Over the course of these sessions, four bills were reviewed for the forthcoming 1978 legislature session: one to create a state office of rural health; one from the Kentucky Academy of Physician's Assistants, addressing physician assistant licensing; one from the Kentucky Nursing Association that would address the licensing of nurse practitioners; and one that would generally define certification requirements for a variety of health care professionals. The attendees voted in favor of each of the bills and agreed to work together, both through KPCA and their own institutions, to ensure the bills' passage.

This first meeting of the KPCA was seen to be a rousing success. Bailey was satisfied with the work they were starting to accomplish, saying, "Now we can focus our energies on working with the executive and legislative branches and not on mending fences in our own ranks." Other local medical professionals agreed with him. Jessie Smith, a comptroller at Louisville Memorial Primary Care Center, said, "We have to stick together or we won't survive. We must be heard to get the laws passed that we need, and an association is a much better way to accomplish this than the piecemeal approach." From the legislative point of view, the association was equally successful. David Bolt, the program coordinator of Health and Child Development in the Kentucky Development Cabinet, said of the KPCA, "They do have the capability to speak as a group to the state legislature, they are legitimate and becoming accepted...we plan to call on them for background and data and consultation on primary care issues."

As successful as their work on the certification problem was, this was only the most immediate goal of the KPCA. Their future plans would include continuing to share expertise between the members, arranging continuing education on the development and management of primary care centers, coordination in recruiting practices for health professionals in Kentucky, and forming relationships with health systems agencies at the government level. Bailey served as an active Chairman, sending a steady stream of informational memos and legislative updates to the organization's members. He found about 80% of his work on the association happened during the times the Kentucky Legislature was in session—and found himself more and more working with the members of the legislative branch to bring about positive change for health care in the state and region. This would prove to be only Bailey's first taste of working in the political system; in 1979, he turned his attention beyond the KPCA to the legislature itself, and entered the Democratic primary as a candidate for the state legislature.

CHAPTER SIX

POLITICAL YEARS: DECIDING TO RUN

Benny Ray Bailey's work with setting up the East Kentucky Health Services Center would in many ways serve as an introduction to his entrance into the political world, even if that wasn't his primary intent at the time. His early work in the senate on the coal severance tax issue would follow a similar pattern.

The years of work Bailey had done with bringing health care to the rural counties of eastern Kentucky were also a training ground for his future political involvement. The various fund raising trips he took—both when he was working with Ray LeRoux from ALCOR and when he did his 1972 fund raising for the East Kentucky Health Services Center clinic— gave him a solid foundation for understanding how the political system worked, and how it could be used to benefit his people. When he was doing fund raising, Bailey found that a lot of the big companies he approached about grants would turn him down, saying they only gave money to organizations in the places they did business. This struck Bailey as just one more iteration of the national trend to dismiss the people who lived in Appalachia. After all, the largest gathering of financiers outside of Wall Street was in Letcher

County, a south-east county of Kentucky that was on the Virginia border. The city of Jenkins in this county was where investors had met to divvy up the coal fields prior to mining. Even outside this hotbed, the eastern Kentucky region was within 500 miles of 70-80% of the financiers in the country, and in a similar range to the majority of the nation's population. In that respect, Kentucky had similar struggles to West Virginia: in the center of everything but still largely ignored by businesses when they looked for places to give grants and make investments because they saw the local population as uneducated hillbillies and never took the time to see through popular stereotypes.

Bailey did manage to break through those stereotypes at times when he was looking for funding for the Knott County clinic. It has been said before that he was a born salesman; when he could meet with those who controlled the money face to face, he could show them without a doubt that there was more to Appalachia than Green Acres or the Hatfields and McCoys. This was in large part because Bailey had a winning combination of charm and intelligence. He would present detailed plans outlining, not only why eastern Kentucky deserved better access to medical care, but also how his clinic would employ a revolutionary new approach to rural primary care, providing accurate statistical figures and cost analysis data that made the corporations sit up and pay attention. Even in the early stages of the clinic, when there was nothing to back up the viability of the plans Bailey and Stumbo had sketched out but their own insistence that it was a good idea, they were able to convince significant donors to contribute to the project. Once the Knott County clinic was up and rolling and had clearly demonstrated an ability to not only provide the region with excellent health care but to be self-sustaining—and to do everything without taking advantage of any federal funds—more and more people from a wider radius began to notice Bailey's impressive work.

Though Bailey and Stumbo's early work on the clinic kept a tight focus on serving the eastern Kentucky region of Appalachia, they thought of it as a nationwide model from the very beginning. They believed their approach to primary care could revolutionize the way medical work was done in rural communities of all stripes. Group practices, like the one set up in Knott County, gave more comprehensive health care options to the residents of rural communities who would otherwise have to travel significant distances to gain access to traditional medical institutions. The emphasis on preventative medicine was also a new angle for rural healthcare providers. Previously, there hadn't been enough resources available to Knott County residents to do things like health screenings or regular check-ups that could catch problems before they could escalate into major issues that were costly to treat. By educating members of the community about how to better take care of their own long-term health and involving the family in treatment and prevention, the system established at the Knott County clinic greatly lessened the strain placed upon the limited resources available to the region—and though each individual rural community would have to tweak these methods to suit their area, both Bailey and Stumbo believed it could do the same elsewhere in the country.

As the East Kentucky Health Services Center grew, its success began to attract nationwide attention from others who believed, as the clinics founders did, that this model could work in a range of different communities. The inclusion of the EKHSC in the Horizons on Display Bicentennial program was a big step in raising national awareness of the clinic's work in Appalachia. In 1976, the Horizons on Display committee selected the Knott County clinic as its model program for rural health care. The official American Revolution Bicentennial Commission movie, We Hold These Truths, featured a ten-minute segment on the clinic and its work. WNET, the PBS flagship station operating out of New York, released a documentary entitled No Place Like Home narrated by Ms. Helen Hays; the Knott County clinic was the only rural program featured in that documentary. The NBC two-hour documentary Health Care in America, narrated by C. Everett Koop, also featured the clinic. Bailey and Stumbo were also the featured in People Magazine twice, and the clinic was also covered in article in Readers Digest, AMA News, Modern Medicine Magazine, The New York Times, The Washington Post, and The AMA Journal. The more attention was focused on the Knott County clinic, the more the model established there seemed like a viable option for improving primary care delivery elsewhere in the country—and the more it seemed as if Bailey's ideas could have a broader reach. Running for a seat in the state's legislature was a logical next step for taking those ideas to a broader audience where they could potentially have a more immediate and far- reaching impact.

Benny Ray Bailey had thought about politics his entire life. As he would say, "The whole world is politics if you're social, if you're meeting people." That viewpoint on the political system would prove to be one of the things that would make him so successful in his early bids for office, ultimately making him a refreshing voice for change on behalf of Kentucky's eastern coal counties. In his work for the clinic throughout the 1970s, Bailey demonstrated great skill in getting people to work together toward a common goal and an ability to convince people from very different economic situations that this work could be in everyone's best interest. As an administrator for the Knott County clinic, this meant aligning the goals of people within the community— many of whom lived at or below the poverty line—with those of the wealthy corporations and businessmen the clinic needed on their side to get the operations up and running. With the Kentucky Primary Care Association, it meant aligning the needs of various health care professionals to be amenable to the members of the legislature so that an issue which had been long- debated could finally be passed. Despite the details, Bailey's affable demeanor made him friends and allies wherever he went. He showed an exceptional talent for finding common ground between groups even when none seemed possible. The political sphere was a logical place for him to apply these talents.

If you ask Benny Ray Bailey why he got into politics, he'll give you a very short answer: severance tax. This issue had been at the forefront of the Kentucky legislature's concerns for about a decade when Bailey made his entrance into the political arena in 1979, and was especially important for the relatively poor counties of Kentucky's eastern coalfield, including Bailey's home county. For someone unfamiliar with the political and economic background of the region, a bit of history is required to truly understand why the severance tax issue was so pressing as the Kentucky legislature prepared for its 1980 session.

The eastern Kentucky coalfield is a part of the larger Central Appalachian bituminous coalfield, which stretches across all or parts of 30 Kentucky counties as well as areas of Ohio, Tennessee, Virginia, and West Virginia. It covers the region from the Allegheny Mountains in the east, across the Cumberland Plateau to the Pottsville Escarpment in the west. This region, now known primarily for coal, was once dominated by family farms; indeed, until surface mining became a common practice in the 1940s and 1950s, this area was largely known for being an agricultural area; in fact, eastern Kentucky became a major player in the coal industry only after World War II.

The first coal was discovered and used in the area that would become Kentucky as far back as 1750, when Virginia explorer Thomas Walker found some during an expedition to the unsettled region of British North America to the west of the Allegheny Mountains. Walker used his discovered coal to heat his campfire; commercial production of coal in the Kentucky area wouldn't happen for another 70 years, when the first commercial coal mine opened in Muhlenberg County, a western county, in 1820. Known as the McLean Drift Bank, this first coal mine was located near Green River and Paradise. The majority of the early coal produced in the state came from the western coalfields, as opposed to those in the east. The terrain in the western half of the country was more amenable to the extraction and transportation of the resource. By the mid- 1800s, the state of Kentucky was producing around 100,000 tons of coal a year, all of which was mined from the western coalfield.

The first commercial coal mine in the eastern coalfield was opened in Betsy Layne in Floyd County in 1900. The production from the eastern coalfields would have its ups and downs during the first half of the twentieth century, largely resulting from changes in demand brought about by global factors. Production was bumped up in the 1910s to meet the demand for energy prompted by World War I. The coal companies that came to the region in these early years of the century built cities for their workers near the mines rather than using local infrastructure, which was largely still aimed at an agrarian rather than an industrial economy. Though the eastern coalfield was being mined at this point, most areas of Knott County and its neighboring communities were still out of the coal industry's reach. The landscape of mountains separated by narrow valleys made it incredibly difficult to extract minerals from the region; though there were a few underground mines in Knott County in the early 1900s, they were predominantly situated along the border with Perry County to the west. As was common at the time, the miners working the eastern coalfield in Kentucky stayed isolated within the coal company cities, shopping at the company store with company scrip, their livelihoods entirely controlled by the coal companies and unconnected to the culture of the rural towns scattered through the hills.

Though they were often referred to as mining camps, the towns established by the mining companies were not ramshackle operations but rather quaint towns, not only homes and a company store but also movie theaters, bowling alleys, even public pools. The town of Wheelwright was founded in Floyd County in 1916 by the Elk Horn Coal Company (it was named for Jere H. Wheelwright, the company's president at the time) was the first town in America where every house had indoor plumbing. These company towns provided for the needs of the miners and their families—at least, as long as the miners were employed by the company. When workers were fired, they also lost their homes; when mines closed, the companies that owned them abandoned the towns, allowing them to fall into disrepair. Even when the mines were doing well, the workers were essentially trapped into their roles, and grew overly dependent on the coal industry to take care of them. There was no point in being an entrepreneur when the only stores in a town were run by the coal industry. For most people, the only way to find employment outside the coal industry was to move away from home.

The white collar jobs that did exist in the coal industry were held almost exclusively by outsiders; the ones who did the backbreaking work in underground tunnels, conversely, were almost exclusively locals.

The Great Depression made a bust of the war-fueled coal boom in Kentucky as it did to countless industries across the nation and the world at large. Local miners who were entirely dependent upon the coal companies for their livelihood were hit especially hard by the economic collapse, but this was only the latest in a series of economic catastrophes to hit the state of Kentucky in the early twentieth century. Though the western half of the state saw the more dramatic spike in unemployment numbers at the onset of the Great Depression, eastern Kentucky's rural communities had been plagued by poverty for some years already before it hit. The economy of eastern Kentucky was still focused as much on farming as it was on mineral production, and prices for the state's crops had fallen steadily even through the boom years of the 1910s. Exacerbating the problem, a century of commercial mining had taken its toll on Kentucky's water and land quality, and farmers were finding it more difficult to grow enough food to support themselves. In 1919, the ratification of the Eighteenth Amendment imposed prohibition, putting an end to Kentucky's thriving bourbon and beer industries. The stock market crash in 1929 and the collapse of the coal industry were the final straw that broke the state's economy. In 1927, there were 622 coal mines operating in the state of Kentucky; by the end of 1932, there were only 380, and 24,000 miners had lost their jobs, and many had lost their homes along with them.

The New Deal programs implemented by Franklin Delano Roosevelt when he took office in 1933 altered the landscape of Kentucky more drastically than any other single event in the state's history since it was first settled, though western Kentucky received the lion's share of the work projects and aid. Of the 80,000 Kentuckians who participated in the Civilian Conservation Corps, for example, only about 5,000 were from eastern counties. The FDR Presidential Library lists 41 construction and art projects that were completed in the state of Kentucky through New Deal programs. Of those, only seven were located within the eastern coalfield; only four eastern counties saw work projects, and the infrastructure in that part of the state remained largely undeveloped through the 1930s. The biggest impact of the New Deal on eastern Kentucky came from the reforms made to the coal industry. Mine safety was improved and new controls were imposed on child labor; the spread of United Mine Workers of America organization across the country following the National Recovery Act in 1933 gave the miners more power to fight for better wages and conditions.

The start of World War II kicked the coal industry back into high gear, this time with enough intensity that the eastern coalfield started to put out significant tonnage. When World

War II ended, a paved road system was built into Knott County and other more isolated regions of Appalachia. Railroad tracks were laid down soon after. New equipment developed during World War II changed the way these new mines brought the coal to the surface. Instead of digging narrow tunnels into the sides of mountains and bringing the coal out this way, the introduction of augers and bulldozers to the industry let them remove the land on top of coal seams and access them directly, a process known as strip mining.

Thanks to these developments and the renewed coal market, the eastern coalfield in Kentucky was producing as much as the west by the end of the 1940s; Knott County alone was producing 1.5 million tons of coal a year by that point. The county population was at its highest during the '40s and '50s, peaking at just over 20,000.

Strip mining was less labor intensive than other mining methods, letting them extract more than twice as much coal per worker; it was also safer for the miners, who no longer had to work in slender tunnels under tons of rock. From the perspective of eastern Kentucky's residents, though, strip mining's drawbacks far outweighed these advantages. Strip mining sometimes removed entire mountaintops, or large swaths of the soil and vegetation along hillsides, leaving only bare stone in the aftermath where nothing could grow. Without the natural drainage system, the soil on the mountains had provided, nothing would slow the rain water as it rushed down the slopes, leading to flash flooding in the hollows, where most of the people lived. The region's waterways were filled with debris, the water picking up toxic levels of heavy metals like iron or other by products, manganese and acid. This impacted both the health of the land and of the people who lived on it; instances of chronic heart, lung, and kidney disease increased in counties now involved in mountaintop mining.

As bad as the environmental impact of this new mining technique was, for most of the area's residents the more egregious affront of the coal companies was the fact that they would destroy privately-owned lands without compensating the property owners. Private citizens had no legal recourse against them thanks to an overly loose applications of the rights granted to coal companies by broad form deeds. These deeds allowed landowners to sell the rights to any minerals found underneath their property while retaining ownership of anything on the surface. It was an arrangement that had worked out well for both parties when many of the deeds were sold in the late nineteenth and early twentieth centuries. Many of the landowners in Kentucky's eastern coalfield were descendants of the Scotch-Irish immigrants who'd been given the land in return for their service in the Revolutionary War. The farms and homes on the land had been passed down over the generations; most of the landowners didn't give much thought to the value of the minerals buried beneath the surface, and the coal operators' old methods of extraction were relatively unobtrusive. Strip mining, though, destroyed the land on the surface in the process of extracting the minerals they owned, something the coal companies insisted was within their rights.

Much of the strip mining in east Kentucky was done through the Kentucky Oak Mining Company. The other coal companies operating in Kentucky's eastern coalfield were non-locals, as was more common throughout Appalachia. They quietly acquired the mineral rights to a significant percentage of Kentucky's eastern coal field; one study at the time showed that about a quarter of Knott County was owned by a handful of corporations. The situation was much the same in neighboring counties. Because the mining was progressively destroying the area's land, coal quickly became the only viable industry in the region, making the residents completely dependent on the same people that were destroying their land. As local landowner and coal industry protestor Doris Shepherd said, "It was just rampant rape-and-run...a lot of them, as soon as they filled their pocketbooks, they left; they left us to deal with the problems."

Some people did try to fight the rampant destruction of local lands and private property. There were often accusations of forged signatures on broad form deeds, but these accusations were hard to prove as many of the ancestors who'd signed the deeds were illiterate and simply wrote an "X" in lieu of their signature. Even when the deed was legitimate, current landowners were enraged by the liberal interpretation of the coal companies' rights under the broad form deeds. The Kentucky courts repeatedly ruled in favor of the coal companies when suits were brought against them.

In 1965, Knott County residents formed the Appalachian Group to Save the Land and People to protest the exploitation of broad form deeds. Their public purpose was the organization of peaceful protests, but there were accusations of nighttime sabotage by members. Since coal operators controlled so much of the economy, though, even membership in a protest group could be dangerous. Protestors could have their food stamps or welfare benefits revoked, or could be arrested for impeding the coal companies at protest sites. When a mining company came to raze the land owned by 61-year-old widow Ollie Combs in 1965, she sat in front of the bulldozers and refused to move. Kentucky State Police were ultimately called in to physically carry her away. Pictures of the incident reached national news outlets. The next year, the state legislature passed some restrictions on surface mining, but they addressed only the worst abuses and set some basic reclamation rules. Many local residents felt the new legislation legitimized strip mining more than it curtailed it. Making matters worse, the local residents who worked in the mines were none too happy about the protests and sabotage. For the miners, their main concern was whether or not they had a job that allowed them to feed their family; when members of the Appalachian Group to Save the Land and People had sit-ins on construction equipment to delay the strip mining of private lands, the local miners would often be the first ones to show up and try to force them to leave, siding with the coal companies out of their own necessity, and making it difficult for local landowners to fight back.

Some landowners tried to challenge the deeds in the courts. In 1964, Lotts Creek resident LeRoy Martin sued to prevent the mining of his land. The Knott County Circuit Judge, John Chris Cornett, sided with Martin, ruling that coal companies would have to compensate landowners for damage done to private property during mining; Martin's attorney during that case, Harry Caudill, would end up staying active in the fight against the unfair actions of the coal industry over the next decade. In 1968, the Kentucky Court of Appeals—the highest court in the state at that time—overruled Cornett's ruling, restoring nearly unlimited power to the coal operators. In April of 1970, residents of Clear Creek and Lotts Creek tried taking a different approach, taking the issue to the Knott County Fiscal Court and demanding the prohibition of surface mining on the basis of it being a public nuisance. The Fiscal Court ruled in favor of the residents and banned surface mining, but the state Attorney General, John B. Breckinridge, overruled the decision, declaring that the fiscal court didn't have the authority to legislate strip mining. Landowners in east Kentucky grew increasingly frustrated. Every time they seemed to have gained ground through legal avenues, King Coal's political clout stepped in to cancel it out. To many residents, it was starting to seem like democracy had failed them.

Prior to 1972, there was no tax on coal in Kentucky. A study conducted by The Appalachian Land Ownership Task Force looked at mineral-rich lands in six states, including twelve counties in eastern Kentucky. The study found that, though ten large corporations owned half of the surveyed land in those twelve Kentucky counties, they paid only 11% of the property taxes. A list of the top 25 surface and mineral rights owners in these counties showed that only four paid taxes of $1 per acre or more. Some paid tax rates as low as 3/100 of a cent per acre. In 1972, Pike County Judge-Executive Wayne T. Rutherford brought the idea of a severance tax before the legislature, suggesting that counties be allowed to tax the coal extracted from their land. This law failed to pass. Some of the counties starting imposing local taxes on the coal operators at a rate of ten cents per ton until a new bill, proposed by Governor Wendell Ford, implemented a state severance tax, stopping the county taxation. A rate was established of 4.5% of the gross value of the coal when it was sold. It was up to the state how this money would be spent, however. From the first year the tax was implemented, the question of how the tax should be divided was a point of contention. Counties wanted to be able to use the taxes the way they saw fit, and coal producing counties believed they should receive compensation proportional to the amount of minerals being extracted from their land. Instead, the state was designating much of the severance tax income for specific projects, like road improvement—and then failing to carry out these projects equally across the state. Once again, the people who had built up the coal industry in Kentucky through their land

and hard work felt as though they were being ignored by their democratic system.

It was the severance tax issue that prompted Benny Ray Bailey to ultimately run for office. As he pointed out in an interview with The Floyd County Times, "It doesn't make sense for the person who owns the land to pay tax on it while the person who owns the coal, where all the value is, pays none." In his mailings, he said, "Our area needs and deserves a higher return of the coal severance tax collected in our counties. Less restrictions on the use of this money will allow us to concentrate on building and maintaining our roads."

The prominence of unions in Kentucky meant that the state legislature typically leaned democratic, at least in the counties of the eastern coalfield which made up Bailey's 29th district (which encompassed Knott, Perry, Floyd, and Martin counties in 1979). Later, Breathitt and Johnson County were added and Martin and Perry were dropped). When Bailey decided to run for office, he knew that his main competition would be in the democratic primary in May. In addition to the severance tax issue, Bailey planned to cut back on the bureaucracy, making the government better, not bigger. He also had thoughts for reforms in the education system, with plans to give better support to classroom teachers to encourage them to stay in the area. Housing programs for the elderly and further development of the coal industry were other talking points in his initial campaign. Bailey earned the endorsement of several key groups, including the United Mine Workers of America, the Communications Workers of America, and the Kentucky Education Association. Through these endorsements and his thoughts on the key issues facing his constituency, Bailey won the democratic primary in May of 1979, and went on to run unopposed in the November general election.

The Kentucky legislature was a part-time commitment, meeting 60 days every two years ("Most people say we'd be in better shape if it was two days every 60 years," Bailey would sometimes joke). Bailey stayed on as the part-time administrator of the East Kentucky Health Services Center after he won the seat in the Kentucky state legislature.

In 1980, the Kentucky Legislature met at Kentucky Dam Village State Resort Park to organize themselves for the upcoming session and to elect legislative leaders. The legislative leadership appointed all legislators to committees to determine the fate of all legislation. The Appropriations and Revenue Committee was the budget committee which determined how money was going to be raised and how all state money was to be spent.

In the summer of 1979, John Calhoun Wells, a friend of Benny Ray's from Auxier in Floyd County, arranged a meeting between Joe Prather (the incumbent President of the Senate who was running for re- election), Joe Wright (a Senator from Breckinridge County who was running for President Pro Tem of the Senate), and three freshman senators from Eastern Kentucky. Benny Ray Bailey was one of those senators, along with John Doug Hays (the newly-elected

State Senator from Pike County) and Charlie Berger (who would be the newly elected senator from Harlan County). This meeting was held at a motel in Whitesburg, and at it, the three freshman senators agreed to support Prather and Wright if they would place all three on the Appropriations and Revenue Committee. In this way, three new senators gained appointments to the most powerful committee in the Kentucky State Senate.

Benny Ray would continue to serve on this committee for his entire 21-year career in the Senate, and chaired the committee in 1998 and 1999.

In Kentucky, prior to 1980, the Governor was all powerful. The Governor would appoint legislators to committees, select the legislative leaders, and pretty much set the legislative agenda. In the mid and late 1970s, a group of senators led by John Berry, Ed O'Daniel, Lowell Hughes, Ed Ford, Danny Meyer, David Karem, Nelson Allen, Mike Moloney, and others began to push for "legislative independence." This group, called "the Black Sheep" by the press corps, offered themselves for leadership positions during the 1980 organizational session.

John Y. Brown, who was elected Governor in 1979, publicly stated that he supported some legislative independence and took a hands-off policy in the legislative leadership races. While some say he wasn't interested, Benny Ray stated that gubernatorial interference in the legislative leadership elections in 1980 would have been fiercely resisted. Ultimately, it would have likely resulted in a stinging early defeat for the newly-elected governor. "John, Doug, Charlie and I aligned ourselves with 'the Black Sheep' from the beginning," Bailey would later say. "We would not have been influenced by appeals from the Governor. The legislative independence movement in the legislature was too far along to be stopped. An old saying applies here: 'You can't put toothpaste back in the tube.' The legislature, led by 'the Black Sheep,' was not about to give up what little independence they had gained." The new leadership of the Senate in 1980 reflected the gains of the Black Sheep had made in the preceding decade in the area of legislative independence.

Bailey's pride in his home shines through when he talks about the region's relationship with coal. He points out that Kentucky helped to fuel the industrial revolution, but never saw the positive aspects of it, like the jobs and the infrastructure development. When the companies he approached during fund raising told him they had no interests in the area, he would say, "Let me bring you to Jenkins and show you the graves of the boys who died at eighteen, nineteen, working for you." The region had spent decades almost exclusively dedicated to mining coal, and the landscape showed the scars of it. He thinks of other states that have capitalized on their natural beauty, like Colorado out west, which drew people with the appeal of rocky vistas and skiing slopes and built a thriving economy around it. The rugged mountains of Kentucky had a similar beauty and could attract the same kind of tourism if they'd been left intact. Instead, the strip-mined peaks were reduced to bleak rock. Though strip mining was safer, accidents still happened, and these tragedies colored people's perception outside the region. Bailey knew he could help make his region a place people would want to come to and live, work he started when he established the clinic and now could continue in the legislature.

Bailey knew he wanted to revise the severance tax policy, reducing the restrictions placed on the spending by special programs at the state level. Given the lack of roadway improvements that had been undertaken in Floyd County, Bailey found it "shocking" to find that there is $185 million in the energy road fund, which is funded with coal severance tax.

A delegation from the Little Mud Creek area brought up a road in their area that was so bad it had recently been given an inspection by state officials, though they were still waiting to see any action to fix the problems the inspector had noted. As with many of the government programs that dictated how coal severance money would be spent, citizens were often left wondering just what that substantial sum of money was being used for; as far as they could tell from the state of roads in their county, none of it had been filtered their way. The Little Mud Creek delegation brought a signed petition with them to this meeting that asked for more attention to be paid to their roadways, a move that Bailey commended. "Preparing a petition, circulating it for signatures, then presenting it is real participation in the government," he said to reporters after the meeting. Aside from the opinions of his constituents about the various issues discussed in the meeting, the takeaway from this discussion was that the residents of Floyd County were invested in their government. They wanted their democracy to start listening to them and working for them. The stereotype of the uninterested and uneducated hillbilly—one which Bailey had long known to be fiction—was thoroughly busted by Floyd County's response during this courthouse meeting. The county had high expectations for what their government could do for them—and Bailey had equally lofty goals to bring them that attention they'd so long deserved, and so long been lacking, as he entered his first legislative session.

When he was elected to the legislature in November of 1979, Bailey was one of three freshman senators from the eastern counties, the other two being Charles W. Berger (of Harlan) and John Doug Hays (from Pikeville). There were two other freshman senators from other areas of the state, as well. Fibber McGhee was from Louisville and the other was Jim Bunning from North Kentucky, who is now a Baseball Hall of Fame member. The three men from the East Kentucky coal fields shared a similar goal of bringing more money back to their home communities by revising the state's use of severance tax money. Bailey believed an equitable tax distribution plan was the best hope for the eastern Kentucky region going into the future. "Our people won't continue to support a system that keeps them poor," he told reporters at the start of the session.

Berger agreed with him, adding, "We have to find out why so much flows out and so little comes back." Seeing a chance to cooperate toward these shared ends, the three freshmen senators stayed in close communication as they began to work toward the upcoming 1980 legislative session.

There were two proposals introduced on the subject of severance tax during the 1980 meeting of the state legislature. One would divide all yearly severance tax revenue over a certain trigger point across all coal- producing counties in the state. The trigger point discussed was variously $177 million and $200 million. Considering that was right around the amount the severance tax was expected to take in the next fiscal year, it meant the counties wouldn't be seeing much in the immediate future from this proposition. This proposition was essentially counting on another coal boom to increase revenues going to the individual counties. The other proposal would distribute half the severance tax money collected to the coal counties, exempting the portion already committed to other projects.

This proposal would mean it was in the coal counties' best interest to reduce the existing commitments on the severance tax money, which aligned with the goals of state finance officials. Laws passed in 1978 determined the use of much of the severance tax money, including $34 million earmarked for transportation and development projects in the coming year. Freeing up these funds would give the state more fiscal flexibility to help them balance their budget.

Bailey thought how counties spent the coal severance tax money would allow them to better provide services that the counties desperately needed, such as ambulance service and road repairs, without having to go through unnecessary red tape. Representative Bill Weinberg from Hindman agreed with him saying, "We want to cut the bureaucracy and get the money back to where it will benefit the people it is supposed to. We want the local officials who were elected to do a job to get money so they can do the job."

Even though he was a newcomer to the official realm of politics, Bailey had experience dealing with people, and he knew that the best way to get what you want was often to give someone else what they were after. In a January 1980 article entitled "Coal Counties May Make a Deal for Bigger Chunk of Severance Tax," Bailey said on the severance tax, "At this point it's the only issue I'm interested in. I can't think about the governor's other programs till I see how he's going to treat the severance tax issue." He and the other senators were still playing their cards very close to their vests when it came to their potential support of the governor's education plans; in the same article, he said he wasn't yet committed on anything.

The legislature agreed not to propose any bills on the matter until they'd had a chance to talk with the governor about his plans. In early 1980, Brown met with a group of lawmakers from the state's coal counties, including both the representatives in the legislature and the judge- executives of the various counties. The representatives stressed to the governor that the severance tax was the top priority in the eyes of most coal counties.

They had no problem supporting their state government; the problem was they didn't feel they were getting adequate support back. Since coal was the only industry in many of these counties, preventing them from gaining access to the taxes levied on it deprived them of any viable source of funding.

There were two bills passed by the Kentucky legislature on the topic of severance tax in March of 1980. Legislators from coal- producing states were divided on the bills. House Bill 968 extended the severance tax to all minerals extracted from the land at the same 4.5% rate applied to coal. While amendments that would have added exemptions to the bill were overwhelmingly defeated, the bill passed by a margin of 21-9. The coalfield legislators were still divided on the bill. John Doug Hays, one of Bailey's fellow freshman senators from the eastern coalfield, praised the bill for expanding the state's potential revenue sources.

Benny Ray Bailey was one of the senators who voted in favor of both HB 968 and HB 970. He admitted that the bills weren't a perfect solution to the issue of mineral severance tax distribution, but they accomplished what he'd been hoping to achieve in his first legislative session—a better plan for compensating coal producing counties for the minerals taken out of their land. By eliminating special programs, the bill gave counties more freedom to spend the severance money where it was most needed, rather than making them wait for approval of the state. In general, Bailey felt the two bills passed on March 28, 1980 would give his area a better hope for the future, letting them fix some of the county's long- standing problems, like the issue of rural roads and reliable ambulance service.

The severance tax issue as it had been decided in March of 1980 was not a perfect solution, and would be revised in future sessions, as some senators had predicted. It was certainly not the sum total of what Bailey hoped to accomplish during his first four-year term as a state representative. It was, though, a good start toward making the change in Kentucky's state government that Bailey and his fellow senators knew was in order. As a freshman senator, Bailey hit the ground running in the winter of 1980; his work on the severance tax issue was just the tip of the iceberg. January of 1980 also saw him named to the budget committee and the Health and Welfare committee, and made the vice chairman of yet another committee—a rare level of success for a first-time senator.

This early success was the result of his political savvy, developed over years of working in fundraising and administration, as well as his natural instincts of how to use the system to his advantage, and how to convince those around him that cooperation could be in everyone's best interest.

In September of 1980, Benny Ray Bailey — along with State Representative Bill Weinberg— were able to take a check for $128,685.35 to the Knott County Fiscal Court. This was the county's share of severance tax allocations from the 1980-81 fiscal year. It was the first check distributed through the Local Economic Assistance program that had been passed by the General

Assembly earlier that year. Bailey had represented the senate in the process of working out this program, which would send $700 million back to east Kentucky over the next decade.

Bailey said of the Local Economic Assistance program in an interview with The Troublesome Creek Times, "Now, once again, the counties can look forward to how they want to spend their money. What they've been getting is script. They had the mistaken idea they were getting money, but they weren't. Actually, the coal counties gave up nothing. They'll get back more directly the first year under this new formula than they got in the last four."

Though $45,000 of the money was already committed to the Knott County Rescue Squad so they could get a new fire engine, that was an allocation decision made by the county, not imposed by a state government agency— and the rest of it could be used however the county deemed necessary. Bailey told the county, "During the next three years of my term, I think we can look forward to a fairer return of our severance tax monies." This had been Bailey's main objective entering into the 1980 legislative term, and now—less than a year after his election—he had already made great strides toward equalizing the distribution of the money, making it far more equitable for the coal-producing counties in the eastern half of the state. It was an early victory for the freshman senator, and with three years remaining in his first term, it was just the beginning of what he would accomplish for his people as their representative in government.

Benny Ray's first legislative session was deemed successful by most observers, including the Capital Press Corps. At the conclusion of the session in April, 1980, the Capital Press Corps voted Benny Ray Bailey the "Outstanding Freshman Senator" for the 1980 Legislative Session.

Deciding to run for political office, leave a successful business, and spend time away from family is difficult. The decision was not made in isolation but in consultation with family and friends. Of course, Benny Ray's family, including his wife Nikki, his sister Aileen Hamilton, and his brothers, Shannon and Doug (Buddy), were a tremendous help during both his campaign and his term, and worked tirelessly on his behalf. Of all his family members, Bailey's mother, Viola Bailey, was perhaps his most ardent supporter. Benny Ray says of her, "My mother was my biggest booster and spent many hours on the phone, visiting relatives and friends and encouraging everyone to register, to vote, and to vote for her son."

Along with his relatives and family, Bailey gives a great deal of the credit for his political success to his friends, both those who encouraged him and those who worked on his campaign. Many of them worked every day of the campaigning up to Election Day and then worked all twelve hours the polls were open so they could encourage every single voter to vote for Benny Ray Bailey.

These people formed a formidable political organization. They were John Pumpkin Combs, Estil Riley, Calvin Manis, Opal and Manus

Halcomb, Ken Terry, Anna Mullins, Frank
Turner, Curt Gayheart, Astor Campbell, P.G.
Gorman, Noah Cornett, Ken Terry, George
Campbell, Roy Campbell, Ken Colwell, Mack Miller, Bill Virgil Johnson, Homer and Mary Hall,
Mack Little, Georgia Hamilton, Sid Triplett, Levi
Johnson, Grover Johnson, Elmer Ray Johnson,
Talt Johnson, Luther Johnson Sr., Luther Johnson Jr., Claude Johnson, Gene Booth, Cora
Booth, Jim Tackett and Hannah Tackett, Bobby
Tackett, Curt and Oma Tackett, , Nokomis and
Mellie Moore, Earl and Hannah Meade, Johnny
Racky, Tommy Hall, Freddie Hall, Doug Frazier,
Roy Frazier, Ed Patton, Sr., Ed Patton, Jr., Herl
Stumbo, Willie Moore, Harlass Hall, Lawton Allen, Sid Allen, Joey Bolen, Jimmy Castle, Hammer Lovely, Frankie Francis, Eugene Howard,
Bolton Martin, Vernon Salisbury, Hubert
Halbert, Julius Moore, T Model Slone, Raymond
Griffith, Sr., Raymond Griffith, Jr., Bide Click,
Tommy Crum, George Hall, Jr., Roy Nelson,
Chester Layne, Roy Smock, Clyde Justice, Holly
Hamilton, Mathew Stephens, Clell Stephens,
Henry Shepherd, Palmer Frasure, Homer Hamilton, Sterling "Porky" Tackett, John B. Tackett,
Bill Reynolds, Bub Reynolds, Joe Wheeler Lewis,
Yvonne Stumbo, James R. Allen, Benny
Sheperd, Irwin Shepherd, Albert Shepherd, John
Caudill, Grady Stumbo, Gerald DeRossett, Willie
Slone, Willis Slone, James Hicks, Rant Slone
Shelby Gayheart, Harold Mullins, Tommy Hall,
Delmar Slone, Talmadge Vanderpool, Mr. And
Mrs. Odas Greene, Estil Honeycutt, Bill Potter,
Ollie James King, Kanawha "K" Hall, Palmer
Harris, Fess Hall, Junellen Mullins, Morris

Shepherd, Cova Perkins, Eugene Slone, Charles Slone, Joel Combs, Charles Cornett, Leslie and Marie Cornett, Albert and Irene Cornett, McKinley Messer, Harlos Watts, Jim Jones, John Vernon Jones, Arthur Jones, Jr, Irene Hays, Amos Nickles, Earl D. Ousley, Delmar Slone, Janet Slone, Jimmy Clyde Nichols, Leonard Nichols, Curtie Hall, Benny Slone, Ralph Slone, Danny Pigman, Doug Hayes, Sammy Wells, Ray Wilcox, Larry Goble, Tom Lafferty, Tommy Lafferty, Jerry Lafferty, Chester Gibson, Bill Wells, Burl Shepherd, Buster Music, Doc Nichols, Dillard Johnson, Preston Nichols, Robert Hall, Carroll Fugate, Ellis Slone, Wilder Caudill, Homer Chapman, Piney Pratt, Truman Back, Alfred Taylor, Ary Hollifield, Fred Conn, Ray Hamilton, "Big" John Goble, Tracy Stumbo, Cledis Stephens, Red Stephens, Burl Scott, Phil Jenkins, Bruce Patton, Chester Gibson, Joe Fields, Kerman and Stella Young, J.P. Pratt, Donald Layne, Bryant DeRossett, Earl D. Ousley, Charles Hackworth, Dickie Martin, Buddy Slone, Alice Whitaker, Don Fugate, Ken Colwell, Ellis Grigsby, Junior Leedy, Ray Calhoun, Dr. Bobby Hughes, Vernon Bailey, Anna Mullins, Paul Bailey, Alfred Ray, Doug Allen, Sid Allen, Norma Turner, Irene Hays, and many others. In Dr. Stumbo's campaign, the results would have been quite different without the enthusiastic support of Julius Martin, and the financial support of B.F. Reed, Howard Norrell, Roy Campbell, George Campbell, and Jerry Fancé Howell.

In later campaigns, Bill Gorman (Mayor of Hazard and arguably the best Mayor in Kentucky) and his brother, L.D. Gorman (who continues to be involved in every civic improvement project in Perry County) were very good and vocal supporters. When Breathitt County was placed in District 29, Mike Stidham, Dean Spencer, Jerry Howell, Dr. Turner, Treva Turner, and Jeff Turner were great supporters. Other great supporters included Ray Preston, Rick Preston, and their mom and dad. Jimbo, Billy Jo Hill and John Henry joined when Johnson County was added to the District.

The above individuals, along with many others, deserve all the credit for the election of Benny Ray Bailey.

CHAPTER SEVEN

THE STATE SENATE:

Benny Ray Bailey described arriving at the first day of the 1980 General Assembly to a reporter in 1995. "I had never been in the senate chambers," Bailey explained. "I didn't know if there was a 'special' procedure to get into the Senate and all I saw was a lady giving out passes." Those turned out to be passes for observers. Someone recognized Bailey and led him to the Senate floor, but if that hadn't happened, Bailey said, "I would have answered my first roll call from the gallery." It's an anecdote that displays why Bailey's political career was so successful, not only the tone of self-deprecating wit but the fact that he was an outsider in the political landscape, a native son of Eastern Kentucky whose sole political ambition was the best possible outcome for his region.

Bailey served as the State Senator for Kentucky's 29th District for 21 years, from his election in 1979 until he lost the democratic primary in May of 2000. In 1984, he was named the Chairman of the Senate Health and Welfare Committee, a powerful position that, according to Mark Chellgren of the Associated Press, "Allowed him to have a greater influence on human services in the state of Kentucky than any other single individual in the government for the past two decades." Of the three bills Bailey authored and is most proud of, none lost a vote in the house or the Senate, especially impressive when you consider the partisan environment of the legislature through the '80s and '90s. Part of his success as a legislator was due to his ability to vary his tactics to suit the situation. He was equally comfortable using sweet reason to convince his colleagues to pass bills as he was using strong arm tactics, putting the weight of his political clout behind his words—a weight that grew the longer he served in the state senate. Using this combination of tactics, many of Bailey's bills sailed through their legislative sessions with virtually no amendments and minimal discussion.

One of the bills Bailey authored—the Health Care Reform Act of 1990—was one of the most comprehensive and progressive pieces of health care legislation in the nation; officials from other states would go on to use it as a model for universal health care. Regarded as one of the state senate's most liberal members, Bailey earned a reputation for fighting on behalf of the poor and blue-collar, both within and outside the coal industry that dominated his district's economy. Kentucky journalist Bill Straub called Bailey, "Eastern Kentucky's most competent and influential member of the legislature," citing assets like his strong knowledge of the health care industry and his willingness to "play rough when he has to... [He] is not afraid of taking on distasteful jobs."

The recognition Bailey received from the Capitol Press Corps as the outstanding freshman senator of the 1980 General Assembly was only the first of many accolades the senator would receive throughout his career. He won both Ohio University's Medal of Merit and Indiana State University's Distinguished Alumni Award (the highest honor bestowed by the college's alumni association) during his political years; Ohio University also presented him with an Honorary Doctorate of Public Service, as did Pikeville College in 1998. In September of 1995, a crisis stabilization unit that opened in Breathitt County was named the Bailey Center in his honor. The 24/7 facility was an alternative to psychiatric hospitalization, one of four such centers opened in Kentucky thanks in large part to funding Bailey obtained for the state's mental health care. The University of Kentucky Center of Excellence in Rural Health Care building in Hazard was also named the Bailey-Stumbo Building to recognize Benny Ray's and Dr. Stumbo's contributions to improvements in rural health care.

At the same time Bailey was throwing his hat into the political ring, his Knott County clinic partner, Grady Stumbo, also became involved in state politics. In 1979, Governor John Y. Brown, Jr. appointed Stumbo as the head of the Kentucky Department for Human Resources. When asked why he did accept the post, Stumbo answered, "I felt like I could do something for Eastern Kentucky, a region many times ignored by state government." Like Bailey, he saw himself as representing "that section of Appalachian culture you don't know and have not had contact with." The appointment brought Stumbo to Frankfort at the same time Bailey was embarking on his first term as a state senator.

The Department of Human Resources Secretary was one of the most publicized and criticized officials in the state government (besides the Governor himself). It was also the highest position an Eastern Kentuckian had held in the state government since Bert Combs served as Governor in the early 1960s. This massive department employed over 12,000 people and dealt with a broad array of concerns, which were broken up into four bureaus: Manpower (dealing with jobs), Social Insurance (for unemployment, welfare, food stamps, and similar programs), Social Services (dealing with juveniles, runaways, orphans, and foster children), and the Bureau of Health Services (which monitored each county's health departments). Stumbo described Human Resources as "where good government happens; where government satisfies definite needs of citizens."

Stumbo believed that part of the reason the department had received so much criticism was that it hadn't been completely honest with either the media or the legislature in the past. Like Bailey, Stumbo believed firmly in ethical government. He corrected this tradition of disinformation, testifying himself at legislative hearings rather than sending subordinates and working toward transparency in all his dealings with those who relied on the department's services. His first move as Department Secretary was to reduce the department's staff to save money and make it more efficient.

Other early moves made him a controversial figure early in his term. He cut spending on hospitals and curbed the rising costs of the Medicaid program and de-institutionalized the treatment of the elderly and mentally ill, moves some people saw as attempts to deregulate these industries. These moves were all made in the interest of working under the tighter budget the state government had to make work in the early 1980s. Despite the initial controversy, Stumbo spoke with concerned parties—like the Kentucky Nursing Association and Kentucky Association for Retarded People—and explained the reasoning behind the changes. The perception of him gradually began to shift as lobbyists and citizens alike realized he was focused on the greater health of Kentucky's people as a long term goal—and that he was actually willing to listen to the concerns of those who were affected by changes in his department. Stumbo described his ambitions for the department in a March 1981 article from The Courier-Journal Magazine, saying, "I want to reform the health care industry and get rid of unnecessary restrictions. I want to build community facilities for alternative health delivery systems for the elderly, the mentally handicapped. I want this to become a better managed department." Stumbo understood the concern over budget cuts and policy changes coming out of his department, saying, "I don't mind the heat as long as I get the job done. All I ask is that people give me time and judge me on the results."

While the above statement was true when he said it in 1981, at least one part of it changed over the next two years—Stumbo decided to run for office, specifically for governor, in 1983. Benny Ray Bailey served as the chairman of Stumbo's campaign. Bailey, Stumbo, and the other Mountain lawmakers who'd come in with the 1980 session had made great strides already in improving their region's position in the eyes of the government, earning the nickname the Hindman Mafia for their unified agenda. Having an Eastern Kentuckian serving as governor, though, would enable them to do even more for the long-neglected region.

However well Stumbo knew the ins and outs of government, he could not compete financially with the millionaire candidates he ran against. He lost the 1983 election by two percentage points, despite spending only about 15% of what the other two candidates in the race spent, and ended up with nearly $300,000 of debt for his troubles, most of which was in personal loans.

Following Stumbo's unsuccessful bid for governor, Bailey proposed Senate Bill 159 during the 1986 General Assembly in an attempt to reform campaign funding in the state. Rich candidates had gotten into the habit of running "on spec," spending massive amounts of private money on the campaign with the intent of recouping the costs through fundraising events once he'd won the office. Bailey pointed out that the 1987 race for governor was happening on two financial levels: the haves (represented by millionaires John Y. Brown Jr. and Wallace Wilkinson) and the have-nots (Grady Stumbo and Lt. Governor Steven L. Beshear), who had strong platforms on the issues but lacked the massive financial backing it would take to compete against their richer counterparts. Reforming campaign finance regulations would help even the playing field in the political arena.

Several themes emerge from looking at Senator Bailey's legislative career as a whole. The strongest is his desire to equalize the attention paid to all of Kentucky's counties, which had traditionally been skewed in favor of the more urban counties, often ignoring the needs of the state's rural residents. When Bailey was elected to the Senate, the road system in Eastern Kentucky was far less developed than that in the western half of the state. By June of 1980, Bailey had organized a meeting between then- Governor John Y. Brown, Jr. and residents of Martin and Floyd Counties to discuss the reconstruction of a key road in the area. Building up the infrastructure that would make Eastern Kentucky appealing to businesses was a major concern during Bailey's tenure in the legislature. This started with getting the counties of the 29th District their fair share of funding under state programs that had in the past often neglected counties like Knott and Floyd in favor of the state's urban areas. Equity in the voices that were heard in the state government was another concern of Bailey's. This often went beyond raising the profile of the coal counties in Frankfort; in a time when the power was shifting from the Democratic caucus to a more truly democratic balance, Bailey was one of the majority party's senators most willing to extend his hand across the aisle, and he supported and sponsored numerous bi-partisan measures during his tenure.

Of course, Senator Bailey was there to represent the interests of the 29th District— Eastern coal counties like Breathitt, Floyd, and Knott Counties. Programs and services that supported and improved the lives of his district's residents were Bailey's primary goal during his time in the legislature. One of his main goals was to keep the brightest minds of the region from going elsewhere to start their lives. During a speech at the Lees College pinning ceremony for graduating nurses, Bailey told them, "Don't go away— don't leave in search of greener pastures. Stay in this beautiful home place and make it better." Through work with the Senate Appropriations and Revenue Committee, the class of dedicated Mountain legislators (of which Bailey was one member) won funding for a medical residency program at the University of Kentucky that would encourage more doctors to relocate to rural areas; provisions in the 1990 Health Care Reform Act worked toward similar goals: keeping natives who could make a difference in the area long-term.

Bailey's work to make the region better also took the form of coal industry reforms, expansion of social services, and the creation of new jobs. These goals often worked hand in hand. Legislation sponsored or authored by Bailey provided for the construction of several new medical facilities in Eastern Kentucky— both expanding the region's access to health care and bringing in more jobs. Even through the years of lean budgets in the 1980s and early 1990s, Bailey fought to get as much money as possible for his district. A 1985 study showed that Knott County had more children living in poverty than 100 other counties, but ranked first in the percentage of children who were eligible for food stamps and actually received them. This statistic shows the results of Bailey's early work to make sure the indigent of his district were getting access to the services they needed. He continued the work he'd started with the East Kentucky Health Services Center to help more impoverished Eastern Kentuckians to get reliable, affordable primary care. "We need reform in the health care and welfare system," Bailey said, "but we need reform that is headed by talented people who understand the system and have mercy in their hearts for people. What we've got...is people who are trying to reform the system with no talent and no mercy for people. That's a tragedy and a disaster for people who need these services." His years of experience in rural health care meant Bailey had the talent and the knowledge to reform the industry the right way—and his love for his home counties ensured that he would work for the benefit of the people, not his own political gains.

Perhaps one of the most important things Bailey was able to accomplish for the area, though, was to raise its profile in Frankfort and beyond. A poll conducted in 1995 showed that 65% of Kentuckians from other regions thought that Eastern Kentucky deserved more attention from the state government, something Bailey and his fellow Mountain legislators had long been aware of but that those outside the region hadn't spent much time thinking about in the past. As the candidates for governor geared up for the election in the mid-1990s, Bailey and his fellow senators from Eastern Kentucky drafted a 15-page questionnaire for the candidates to fill out. The 73 yes or no questions of the survey were designed to get the candidates' opinions on key points Bailey called rural issues more than mountain issues. Bailey explained the reason for the questionnaire by saying, "Usually they'll court us pretty hard until after the election, and then they'll write us off." Under Bailey's watch, the 29th District would not be written of any longer.

The themes of Bailey's political work were exemplified by the legislation he authored, sponsored, and voted for during his two decades of work in the state senate. This work can be broken down broadly into three categories: Coal reform, health care reform, and cultural and political maneuvers aimed at raising Eastern Kentucky's profile in the minds of the state's governing bodies.

Coal Industry Reforms

Issues like the broad-form deed and severance tax distribution that had prompted Bailey to run for office in the first place continued to be major points throughout his career in the state senate. If you asked him, Bailey would tell you without question he was a coal miner's—more than a coal operator's— candidate. This is not to say he didn't support the coal industry; as the pillar of the economy in Eastern Kentucky, the success of the coal industry was very important to the residents of Bailey's 29th District, and by extension important to Bailey as its representative. He firmly believed in the right of the mine workers and land owners to profit from the coal mined in Eastern Kentucky and fought for a more equitable distribution of the mineral wealth. Curtailing the abuses the area's residents had endured for so long at the hands of the coal industry's largest operators while still allowing the industry itself to flourish was the important balancing act Bailey maintained throughout his legislative service.

The changes made to the distribution of coal severance tax money during the 1980 legislative session were in many ways predicated on the continued success of the coal industry in the state. If the industry had continued to grow and turn a greater profit than before, the counties where the coal was mined would have seen the money they received from the mined coal rising with the tide. Unfortunately, the industry continued to shrink through the 1980s; the eventual payoff the counties of Eastern Kentucky had been hoping for from the reforms never materialized. Never one to shy away from a challenge, Bailey continued to chip away at the severance tax issue throughout his time in the legislature. By the start of the 1990s, Bailey had been in the senate long enough to accumulate the reputation capitol and political clout to again take on the issue of severance tax reform.

Bailey's new proposal was first introduced to the senate in a special session held in August of 1991. When Bailey raised this issue, counties where coal was mined—or counties whose roads were affected by coal transportation—received

12% of the money collected from severance taxes. A bill was introduced by Governor Wallace Wilkinson that would immediately increase the amount sent back to coal counties to 25% of the total severance taxes collected, gradually increase this amount to 50% over the next several years. Bailey argued, instead, for increasing the amount coal counties received to 50% immediately, in an effort to jump- start the rebuilding efforts of those counties. He pointed out that legislation had been approved in the past for gradual increases to as high as 39% of the severance tax money, but that none of those programs were currently being funded.

Lawmakers from non-coal counties were reluctant to accept any of the proposed severance tax legislation. Arguments ranged from an assertion that the special session wasn't the right time to tackle this issue to a flat-out rejection of raising the severance tax at all, with many arguing that increasing the severance tax money received by coal counties would only increase their dependence on the industry.

Severance tax certainly wasn't the only issue on the minds of coal county legislators. The safety of those working in the coal mines was a major issue for Eastern Kentucky. A worker's compensation reform that passed through the legislature in the 1980 session was an unfortunate step back for the state, weakening the rights of blue collar workers to claim compensation for injuries sustained on the job. Black lung was one of the biggest public health issues in the coal counties. This ailment was caused when miners breathed in the coal dust put into the air

during the mining process. Rather than imposing reforms that would make the coal operators
control the dust, preventing black lung from developing in miners, the legislation passed
through the legislature instead made the coal
companies pay for treatment of those afflicted by
black lung. What was worse, those who'd con-
tracted the ailment had to prove their breathing
capacity was diminished by 10% before they
could even apply for compensation. Bailey argued, instead, for a stricter enforcement of the
law controlling air quality within the mines—a
preventative approach that would improve the
quality of life for miners and greatly reduce the
financial burden of care for those who'd con-
tracted the disease.

Another piece of legislation supported by Senator Bailey looked to bring more equity to the
operator side of the coal industry. Introduced to
the House of Representatives, House Bill 835
would lessen the burden of small operators (defined as those who mined less than 200,000
tons per year) to pay the increased permit fees
brought about by new industry regulations. The
large coal operations were far more likely to be
controlled by outsiders than locals; supporting
small coal operators and helping them stay in
business ultimately helped keep more of the
money in the state.

Perhaps the most important reform to the operations of the coal industry in Eastern Kentucky during Benny Ray Bailey's tenure in the
senate was the imposition of new restrictions on
the broad form deed. For decades, coal operators
had been using these agreements to justify strip-

mining private property in order to access the coal seams beneath. Attempts by property owners to challenge the rulings in the courts were inevitably stymied by coal industry lobbyists; operators were given free rein to destroy the land. In 1988, Bailey introduced an amendment to the state constitution that would finally impose restrictions on the use of broad form deeds. Owners of mineral rights would still be allowed to extract coal, but only using methods that were known in the state of Kentucky at the time that the deed was purchased. Since most of these deeds had been purchased prior to the use of strip mining, it would put an end to the rampant destruction of private property. The amendment passed the legislature and went to a public vote, where it was ratified with the support of 80% of voters.

At the same time, he worked to bring reform to the coal industry, he looked for ways to diversify the region's economy. In 1980, he wrote a letter to Governor Brown asking that he consider Eastern Kentucky as a potential location for synfuel plants. He wrote that it was cruel to exclude the region from "the construction jobs, economic diversification, cleaner transport of synfuels, and area economic development that would accompany the development of synfuel plants in the heart of the nation's coal fields." Bailey went on to say it was ironic the region had to ask for inclusion in the energy industry that had dominated its economy and been "both a blessing and a curse to us." Outside the energy industry, the Health Care Reform Act Bailey brought to the senate in 1990 provided for the construction of new medical facilities, and with them an influx of jobs in the health care industry; other provisions in that legislation expanded access to education so rural Kentuckians could become qualified to fill those jobs.

Eastern Kentucky's complicated relationship with the coal industry had long prevented the region's lawmakers from attempting reforms out of fear that interfering with their operations would hurt the only viable industry they had. The freshman senators from Eastern Kentucky in 1980 were the first to push back successfully and gain some ground for the region. While the power of the coal lobby at every level of the government was dominant, mountain legislators often had to fight through failures to make progress, but their determination yielded powerful results, like the 1988 changes to the broad form deed.

Health Care Reforms

Benny Ray Bailey was one of the state's strongest advocates for affordable and comprehensive health care even before he was elected to the state legislature, and he continued this fight in the State Senate, leaving a legacy of health care reform that would help to make Kentucky's health care laws some of the most forward-thinking of any state's by the mid- 1990s. The fight for equitable and affordable health care would last throughout Bailey's legislative career, with the Omnibus Health Care Bill passed by the legislature in the 1990 session serving as the most significant result of these reform attempts.

Bailey first introduced health care legislation in 1984; the senate approved pieces of this proposal, but not his entire package. In 1986, Bailey introduced an early version of his Omnibus Health Care Reform Act, a 108-page measure co-sponsored by Bailey and Senator Mike Moloney that was the most far-reaching piece of legislation to go before the General Assembly in the 1986 session. Included in the bill was a Medicaid reform that would have set up two competing systems to help hold down ever-increasing health care costs and a health insurance reform that would give families in need one-time catastrophic coverage for emergencies. The bill passed the Senate but stalled in the House and died in a committee without coming to a vote. The provision that likely led to its death was a provision that imposed a 3% surcharge on health insurance premiums that would pay for the bill's other policies. Opponents objected to this provision on the basis that health care is a society-wide measure and should be financed by all of society—an objection that ultimately didn't make sense, considering the same group of people who'd be paying the insurance premium surcharge were the ones who made enough to pay income tax. Though the bill's failure was disappointing, Bailey took it in stride, telling The Courier-Journal, "I guess we're just like Paul Masson wine—we just can't pass a bill before its time."

Bailey was able to use his position as the chairman of the Health and Welfare Committee to piggyback some of the proposals into law when the reform seemed like it would fail. This well-known legislative tactic involves attaching a bill (or part of one) to another as an amendment; the main restriction is that the amendment has to relate to the title of the bill it's being attached to. Bailey systematically re- named any House legislation related to health care that passed through his committee to something suitably generic, permitting some of his health care re- forms a chance to pass through as amendments. Though this kind of political maneuvering was well within Bailey's skill set—and did precipitate some important health care reforms—the sena- tor's ambitions were much broader than piggy- backed amendments. His long-time hope had been to revolutionize the way Kentucky dealt with health care and insurance, especially for rural and indigent populations.

Kentucky had been moving toward better health care legislation throughout the 1980s. It was ranked 20th in the nation in health care in 1988; by the start of 1990, it had moved up the rankings to 16th, but the system was still largely fragmented and spotty in terms of coverage, with some areas, populations, and specialties receiv- ing far bigger budgets and offering far better ser- vices than others. When it came to mental health, for example, the state spent only 19 cents of every $100 of per capita income on pro- grams and care—less than all but five other states.

The health care legislation Bailey introduced in 1990 sought to change all of that in one mas- sive piece of legislation that even his detractors had to admit was genius in its construction, if daunting in its complexity. Introduced in February of 1990 as Senate Bill 239, the bill was referred to as the Health Care Reform Act and proposed a health care system that would be one of the most progressive and comprehensive in the country, significantly expanding access to quality medical care for the state's blue-collar, rural, and indigent populations. Containing more than 25 separate proposals, the bill had seen nearly 50 revisions since Bailey started working on it in the spring of 1989. Among these proposals were measures aimed at attracting doctors to rural areas. The construction of a new $20 million facility for the University of Kentucky's Center of Excellence for Rural Health, located in Hazard, would create new recession-proof jobs in the area while expanding the region's appeal to medical students and physicians; that program would also research health policy and health care delivery, collecting invaluable knowledge on Kentucky's rural populations. An adjustment to the disbursement of Medicaid funds to rural areas to try and convince physicians to work in rural areas of the state. Physicians had historically avoided practicing in rural counties where many of the residents were on Medicaid because they could only receive a percentage of their fees from treating these patients. The Health Care Reform Act proposed a system that would give rural doctors meeting certain conditions an extra 25 cents for each dollar of Medicaid money they received. Another proposal would allow University of Kentucky medical students to complete the last three years of their residency at a rural facility. "Where you do your residency is usually where you do your practice," Bailey pointed out. "This should help us with the doctor shortage in Eastern Kentucky."

The act also addressed the shortage of medical practitioners in rural areas by making it easier for people to become health care professionals. New programs at Hazard Community College would offer Bachelor degrees in medical technology and physical therapy, along with a fast track Master's degree in nursing, increasing the number of nurses with specialized training who could practice in the area. An innovative new program through the University of Kentucky would allow two-year students from any college in the state to transfer into medical technology and physical therapy programs; another program implemented at both the University of Louisville and the University of Kentucky enabled students to complete a Family Practice program in six years after completion of high school. A new form of licensed professional was established in the mid-level health-care practitioner, who would serve in a similar role to the physician extenders used by Bailey and Stumbo's clinic in Knott County. These professionals would be able to deliver basic health care and treat common ailments under the supervision of a physician, expanding the number of patients that could be seen by doctors in areas with limited access to hospitals or clinics. The pharmacy outreach program improved pharmaceutical care in rural areas, putting an emphasis on drug therapy and continuing education for pharmacists.

Another set of programs in the Health Care Reform Act was aimed at providing medical care for the state's uninsured population. In 1990, approximately 700,000 of Kentucky's residents were uninsured, about half of whom were gainfully employed but couldn't afford insurance— the state's "working poor" population. The act established tax credits for employers so that they could provide health insurance to workers and established health care trusts that allowed small businesses to pool their staff, letting them qualify for lower group rates. Changes to the Medicaid program expanded access and changed the amount of reimbursement hospitals could receive. A 1% surcharge on all hospital services would be collected in a fund that would be matched by the federal Medicaid program, generating $67 million. The legislation required hospitals to treat, free of charge, all patients with incomes up to 100% of the poverty income level. The bill was touted as offering "cradle to grave care," with provisions aimed at all age groups, from infants through the elderly.

Prenatal care was extended to cover more women, with Medicaid coverage expanded to include pregnant women and infants to age 1 at 185% of the poverty income level, dramatically reducing infant mortality in Kentucky. Case managers were provided for elderly patients and reforms made to elderly care that aimed to treat patients in their houses instead of putting them in nursing homes.

Providing better health care for the poor also meant building medical facilities in areas that now lacked proper access to services, with attention largely focused on Eastern Kentucky. A new 100-bed mental hospital near Hazard ARH and an 80-bed personal care facility for the mentally ill in Knott County provided much-needed attention for the region's mentally ill, who often found themselves in county jail waiting for one of the state's other mental hospitals to have an opening. Senior citizen centers and day care facilities would also be constructed in traditionally underserved areas under the new law. Not only did these facilities expand access to medical attention, they created recession- proof jobs in many of the areas where employment was hardest to find.

The Health Care Reform Act was approved by the senate on March 2, 1990. Though some questions were asked, there was no significant debate; the bill passed unopposed, with a final vote of 35-0. On March 28, it was passed through the House of Representatives, again unopposed, and sent back to the Senate for concurrence on the single amendment that had been added in the House. When asked why this attempt at reform had succeeded where his past two had failed, Bailey answered, "Maybe I just never could explain it before. I think the bill... has improved every year since 1984." He added, "I think people are getting more and more interested in health care and health care costs."

Despite the sweeping nature of the reforms, the bill passed to relatively little fanfare, largely overshadowed by the sweeping education reforms and drama over hospital regulation that had dominated coverage of the 1990 legislative session. One reporter speculated the lack of publicity concerning Bailey's bill could be due to the fact that "many reporters, editors and media personnel do not understand it." The legislation's incredible detail and innovation—its greatest strengths, in some regards—didn't translate well to headlines and sound-bites. The reform initially seemed to attract more attention outside the state than within it. Trish Riley, the executive director of the National Academy for State Health Policy, said the reform "puts Kentucky in the same league with progressive states that have begun to find creative ways to solve the problems of the uninsured." The nationally-acclaimed public TV program McNeil-Lehrer Report visited Bailey to discuss the legislation, and officials from other states saw the reform as a potential model for health care throughout the nation. In Bailey's native Eastern Kentucky, at least, people understood and appreciated the results of the legislation. He was named 1990 Times Man of the Year, an award given annually to the Knott Countian who made the most positive impact on the area during that year. He'd been recognized the previous year by the Kentucky River Area Development District as the most effective state legislator that region had seen in decades. Bailey's work brought not only rural medical care but positive publicity to Eastern Kentucky, destroying popular misconceptions of the bumbling hillbilly with his revolutionary legislation.

A special session of the legislature was held in 1991. There were several measures on the agenda for this session, not least of which was a Medicaid proposal, constructed by Bailey and supported by Governor Wilkinson, which would expand the program approved by the 1990 General Assembly. Though there were other bills on the docket for the special session, the Medicaid expansion was called "the real story of the session" by political journalists. The bill would create a fund to improve Medicaid coverage, putting $170 million in support over a two-year budget. The bill required nursing homes, doctors, and other health care providers to pay into this fund, where their contributions would be matched by the federal government. The money brought in by this bill prevented the need for sweeping, draconian cuts to the welfare system that would have otherwise been necessary to cope with the state's limited budget. Reactions to the bill from health care professionals was mixed. Jim Judy of the Kentucky Association of Health Care Facilities said, "The concern is you take something this major and try to resolve it in just a few days without a whole lot of debate and study. On the other hand, it sure beats the alternative of cuts."

By the end of the 1992 General Assembly, the health insurance issue still hadn't been resolved. New state governor Brereton Jones introduced a proposal in September of 1992 that would require all businesses to provide health insurance to their workers, with businesses that were deemed to be "vulnerable" becoming eligible for state subsidies. Many small businesses found Jones' plan concerning, and weren't convinced these subsidies would be enough to allow them to pay for the program. In response, Bailey introduced his own plan that outlined a similar program but gave more details about the execution, clarifying what small businesses would have to pay "so we don't scare everybody to death." The main difference between Jones' and Bailey's plans was whether or not the legislation would set rates. Jones wanted to wait and see if free market competition would bring health care costs down before imposing a rate schedule; Bailey's plan called for rates to be set immediately based on the Medicaid reimbursement system. The two proposals were discussed in the Health and Welfare Committee in preparation for the next special session of the whole legislature in March of 1993. Bailey believed immediate control of costs was an essential tenet of any health insurance reform and made it clear no health insurance reform bills would get out of his committee unless it set immediate cost controls. "If we don't do something to control costs," he was quoted as saying, "we can forget about universal coverage."

Bailey had a running disagreement with the two medical schools in Kentucky, the University of Kentucky and the University of Louisville. While everyone seemed to agree that a great percentage of health care needs could be met with primary care providers, the medical schools continued to emphasize the training of specialists. Medical schools routinely paid the highest salaries to specialist and gave them the finest office space and furniture. Being in a state that claims to be the "horse capital of the world," Bailey likened the education of physicians to "training every horse in the world to only run a mile and a quarter as fast as they could then wonder why we couldn't find one to plow." Although both UK and UL gave lip service to their commitment to train primary care physicians, neither school ever made any commitment to these programs.

In May of 1993, Bailey unveiled another plan to ensure coverage for those who couldn't afford it on their own. This proposal would use the individual's income to determine the cost of their health insurance. Those whose income was at least 200% over the poverty line would be required to provide their own coverage; those below the poverty line would have their health care paid for in full. For those who fell in between, their health care cost would be a percentage of the total bill based on their incomes. A Health Care Authority would be funded to make up the difference between what patients could pay and what the doctor charged. This system was supported by recent testimony from Kentucky Blue Cross and Blue Shield representatives who'd stated that about 25% of current hospital costs were used to provide care for the uninsured. The hope for this plan was that it would encourage more Kentuckians to go to the doctor regularly for preventative care. As Bailey said, "Providing primary care for $4 million would probably save $40 million in emergency care at the tertiary level."

The struggle to provide all Kentuckians with affordable health care would continue throughout Bailey's time in the State Senate, with each introduced proposal edging the state one step closer to the ideal of providing everyone with the tools to manage their own health without putting too much strain on the state's budget. A bipartisan bill introduced to the Senate during the 1994 General Assembly that would require government employees to join a statewide health insurance purchasing alliance passed quickly through the Senate, but resurfaced during the 1996 legislative session as insurance rate increases made those reforms non- functional. The Health and Welfare committee met with actuarial consultants in 1996 to discuss the effects of the 1994 reform. A new bipartisan bill introduced in the House during that session (sponsored by Republican representative Ernest Fletcher from Lexington and Eastern Kentucky's Greg Stumbo) would allow insurance companies to charge different rates depending on the individual's health history, age, gender, and occupation—an inequitable system that the reforms through the early '90s had sought to eliminate. On the last day of voting for the 1996 General Assembly, Bailey was able to work out a compromise that would give insurance companies more flexibility without allowing an individual's medical history to influence their premiums. Each new bill edged the state closer to the ideal plan Bailey had envisioned since first introducing health care reform legislation back in 1984— and each subsequent meeting of the legislature brought a new challenge to that progress, whether it was fueled by concern over the state budget or brought about by health care lobbyists.

Through all the back and forth, Bailey remained at the fore-front of the reforms, standing by his guns and fighting for the rights of all Kentuckians to affordable and comprehensive health care.

Certificate of Need Legislation

The debate over Kentucky's certificate of need law started in 1989 and continued through the 1990 legislative session. The Senate's Health and Welfare Committee (of which Bailey was the chairman) had been meeting with their House counterpart since August trying to find an acceptable update to Kentucky's current hospital regulation laws, which imposed restrictions on new services offered by hospitals throughout the state, making them demonstrate verifiable need for the service in the hospital's area before they could be approved for any major equipment or construction expenditures. The intent of this law was to prevent duplication of services in hospitals, but some medical groups—most notably Humana Inc., a company that ran four major hospitals in Louisville—found the law too limiting, and began lobbying for its repeal.

Humana wanted the state of Kentucky to allow free competition in the hospital industry, letting the market dictate what services a hospital offered, and at what price. The Kentucky Hospital Association (KHA), which represented the interests of 111 of the state's 120 hospitals, opposed the repeal of the certificate of need law. They contended that free market competition couldn't work in the health care industry, asserting that access to medical care was a public issue and should be regulated as such. Thus started a bitter battle between these organizations, one which often saw the General Assembly caught squarely in the middle.

There was significant disagreement within the legislature of how to approach the certificate of needs issue from the very start. Two different bills were introduced to the senate early in the session. One from Senator William Quinian would exempt all hospitals from the certificate of need requirement, in essence repealing the state's hospital regulation laws, a proposal that was endorsed by Humana. The other, introduced by Bailey in response to Humana's bid, would retain the control over certificate of needs through the Commission for Health Economics, exempting fewer facilities than Quinian's proposal but also increasing the purchasing limit to $1 million before companies would be required to obtain a certificate of need. Bailey's proposal would ultimately go to the legislature as Senate Bill 68.

The KHA supported Bailey's modifications to the law, as did Alliant Health System (Humana's biggest rival in Louisville, owning Norton Hospital, Kosair Children's Hospital, and Methodist Evangelical Hospital), which had helped Bailey to write the bill in the spring of 1989. Humana, though, considered Bailey's proposal too limiting; the company's Vice President of public affairs, George Atkins, said he agreed with 95% of Bailey's ideas, he opposed the control of services, saying it wouldn't let them do what they needed to do as a company. Humana had been planning on building a medical center in Louisville—a $300 million facility they referred to as their "center of excellence." This new facility would employ somewhere between 3,000 and 5,000 people, according to their estimations.

They insisted that, if they weren't granted an exemption from the Certificate of need law, they would be forced to move this facility to another state with more favorable laws. Alliant's president, G. Rodney Wolford, was willing to compromise on the issue, supporting a repeal of certificate of need regulations in 1992 if there were programs in place to ensure fair competition after the deregulation. Wolford's primary concern was to put an end to the current practice of offering a deep discount to certain insurance companies, resulting in an inequitable system whereby some patients paid twice or even three times as much as others for the same service.

Bailey circulated a proposed amendment to the certificate of need legislation in early January, 1990; this amendment would designate any county with more than 3,000 acute care hospital beds a "national tertiary care center" and make that county's hospitals exempt from the certificate of need regulation. Jefferson County, which contained Louisville and with it all of Humana's hospitals, was the only county in the state that would qualify for the exemption at the time the bill was being considered. Humana said this exemption would be acceptable and allow them to continue operating in the state. But Humana wasn't the only party interested in the outcome of this legislation; the Kentucky Hospital Association found the wording of the amendment too vague, and wanted it to include stronger language regarding tertiary services. Bailey proposed a compromise, which both Humana and the KHA promptly rejected, bringing the certificate of need issue to a stand-still. In response, a frustrated Bailey told The Courier-Journal, "We all know the issue. We know what everybody wants. I don't know if we can find a solution that everybody hates equally."

The compromise process continued following the Humana meeting. Louisville Mayor Jerry Abramson met with Alliant's G. Rodney Wolford and Humana co-founder David A. Jones outside the senate chambers on January 12, 1990, while the legislature was meeting inside. While they were outside striking their deal, Senator Nick Kafoglis introduced his own amendment. This amendment passed. When Abramson returned with the compromise he'd worked out between Wolford and Jones, it was rejected because it conflicted with Kafoglis' amendment that had already been passed. Jones stated afterwards that the committee's decision was a "great first step," but was only the beginning of a longer journey. He also stated his intention to follow the compromise Abramson had worked out, despite its failure in the senate. By the time SB 68 reached the senate floor for a vote, the amendments had made it a drastically different piece of legislation than the one Bailey had originally conceived. The bill was so changed that Bailey voted against it, saying, "It's not my bill. It's been changed substantially and I'm against it." Ultimately, SB 68 passed by a vote of 23-12 after a two-hour debate in which the senate gallery was filled with health care lobbyists. Following the vote, Bailey told reporters, "Don't anybody be confused about this issue. This issue is not about health care. It's about money."

The KHA had not been involved in the hallway negotiations of Mayor Abramson and was against the compromise that had been worked out. By the time SB 68 reached the House of Representatives, the KHA was vocal about its opposition. The bill traveled a rocky road through the House; it escaped its committee with minimum votes, was defeated on the House floor in a tie, then resurrected two days later and approved by a vote of 50-45 to be sent back to the Senate for concurrence on amendments. In the senate, a vote to kill the bill narrowly lost. It was March 30—the final day for passing bills during the 1990 legislative session—that the bill passed both the House and Senate and was sent to Governor Wallace Wilkinson for final approval. Like any good compromise, the bill gave both Humana and the KHA some things that they liked and some things that they hated. It did accomplish the original task of streamlining the process hospitals had to undergo to obtain project or service approval. What had started as a health care regulation bill, though, ended up being more about economic development, as Bailey shrewdly pointed out when the bill first cleared the Senate back in January.

Cultural Legislation

Throughout his life, Benny Ray Bailey was proud of his heritage. Many of his most controversial actions and statements during his time in the State Senate were a result of his advocacy for the cultural traditions of Eastern Kentucky. Bailey's political opponents were not below using common stereotypes about Appalachians, either, in their efforts to undermine his credibility with the voting public. The image of the dimwitted, uncultured hillbilly was so pervasive in popular culture by the time of Bailey's election to the Senate that it made an easy archetype to play off of, however untrue or unfair. This prevailing image was often used to twist Bailey's policies on culture and the arts into negative publicity that often overshadowed the more important reforms to the coal and health insurance industries that were Bailey's true work and legacy as a member of the state legislature.

During the 1980s, a bill came before the state legislature to fund construction of the Kentucky Center for the Arts. Benny Ray Bailey was one of the senators who voted for the bill, which passed into law. The Center for the Arts opened in Louisville in 1983. It served as the home of the Louisville Orchestra, the Louisville Ballet, and the Kentucky Opera, in addition to a host of touring groups and events, even making its political debut when it hosted a debate between Presidential candidates Ronald Reagan and Walter Mondale. The Center provided a great cultural service for the state of Kentucky, and Bailey recognized that. It was not the construction or presence of the building he objected to, but a proposal brought before the legislature in 1990 that would have the state pay for some of the center's operating expenses. What Bailey objected to was the use of public money when the Center could just as easily have paid for their operating expenses by raising the cost of admission, allowing the people who actually used the center to fund it. When talking to the media about the issue, Bailey made a joke about folks who "run around on their tip-toes" and "in their underwear speaking in tongues," a comment that had its source more in the disparity of funding between rural and urban programs than in a desire to dismiss the work of the Center for the Arts.

Unfortunately, not everyone realized his words were meant in jest. Bailey was labeled by certain media outlets as the senator who didn't want to support the arts, a claim that ignored Bailey's initial vote in favor of the Kentucky Center for the Arts. Those who thought of him as someone who didn't appreciate the arts would be surprised to learn about his role in opening the Mountain Arts Center in Prestonsburg. With classrooms for bands or private instruction and a state-of-the- art recording studio in addition to the 1,046- seat theater, this 47,000 square foot center served as a performance space in Eastern Kentucky and a space to preserve Appalachia's musical heritage. Senator Bailey persuaded the government to give the Mountain Arts Center the same percentage of the total budget that was given to Louisville's Center of the Arts. When the center opened in 1996, it became the designated home of the Kentucky Opry and a cultural touchstone for the region.

The truth was, as one Courier-Journal editorial pointed out, Bailey was "as much at home in the Harvard Club as in the general store...an educated, cultured man, as intelligent as he is handsome." To Kentucky's political reporters, this made him something of an enigma—a senator who talked like Eastern Kentucky but was as

143

well-educated as anyone else in the legislature. His support of Appalachian cultural traditions was out of pride for his heritage more than it was a lack of culture. When 48 Hours aired their "Muddy Gut Hollow" episode on CBS in 1989, which gave a sensationalized portrayal of the rural Eastern counties of Kentucky, Bailey was outspoken in his critiques of their portrayal, pointing out that major news shows "have a history of bashing Appalachians and ignoring the contribution of our people and our area to whatever claim America and Kentucky have to greatness." He added that, "we don't eat caviar in East Kentucky, we eat soupbeans. We don't think it is a comment on the intelligence of people in other areas because they eat fish eggs; we don't think it is a comment on our intelligence because we eat soupbeans."

The Appalachian cultural tradition that was perhaps the most misunderstood outside of the region was that of fighting gamecocks. "Muddy Gut Hollow" portrayed a cockfight in the episode, claiming that hundreds of thousands of dollars would change hands in a given night. Cockfighting was illegal in Kentucky; one month and one day after the episode aired, the state police conducted a major raid of the Doty Creek Sports Club in Floyd County, charging 38 people with second- degree cruelty to animals. Despite the timing, state police officers denied speculation that the television program had directly led to the raid. They did say it sped their investigation, which had been going on since the previous summer, when three undercover officers had attempted and failed to infiltrate the operation.

Located in Bailey's 29th District in the Senate (and Greg Stumbo's district in the House) the Doty Creek Sports Club was one of the oldest and largest cockfighting operations east of the Mississippi River. The 100-foot square building was at the top of Sizemore Mountain, three miles off of KY 122. Security was understandably tight at the entrance; newcomers had to be accompanied by a current club member to gain access. The membership ledger confiscated by the police during the raid listed more than 7,000 members, including some from as far north as Michigan and as far south as Louisiana. The confiscated ledger dated back to 1960, though one spectator in the building at the time of the raid told an officer he'd been attending cockfights sponsored by the club since 1936. The building on Sizemore Mountain had been open since 1973, and was referred to in a Courier-Journal article as "a dramatic example of how cockfighting has survived, even in a state where it is illegal."

The 48 Hours episode brought the sport to the forefront of the public's awareness, but for Eastern Kentuckians it was a well-known past- time. Though officially illegal, most Eastern Kentucky police officers had traditionally looked the other way—and the sport had its advocates in the state legislature. Senator Charles Berger of Harlan was referred to by one reporter as the "legislature's patron saint of cockfighting." Berger was open about the fact that he regularly attended cockfights and raised fighting chickens of his own. Greg Stumbo, the House of Representatives' majority leader, was a Floyd County native and was open about the fact that he'd attended cockfights, though he would add, "I've never bet or performed any illegal activity at a cockfight. I don't fight chickens, but I don't see a great deal of harm in the people that do." He told one story of stumbling on a cockfight while he was campaigning for his first legislative race—and working the crowd there, the same as he would anywhere else. His father, Floyd County District Judge Harold Stumbo, was quoted as saying that, regardless of the sport's legality, the people who ran his county's various sporting clubs were by and large "pretty good people."

During the 1980 General Assembly, Bailey and Berger co- sponsored Senate Bill 263, which sought to amend the portion of Kentucky law that defined animals to exclude birds, thereby removing them from protection under the state's animal cruelty laws. It was ostensibly a measure to help farmers control the burgeoning blackbird population; under the current law, farmers would be criminally liable for the deaths of blackbirds on their land, and needed to be able to deal with their problem. "That's the justification for it," Bailey was quoted as saying by The Courier-Journal in a 1980 article, "Now whether it legalizes rooster fighting is probably questionable." The bill was placed on the State Senate's consent calendar and passed 35-1 on March 7, at which point it went to the House of Representatives, where it passed on March 27 by a vote of 69-11. After its passage through the House, Bailey was quoted as saying he hoped then-Governor John Y. Brown, Jr. would sign it into law "before anything is written about it that would cause him to veto it or cause people to start hollering and crying."

Unfortunately for fans of the sport, the hollering and crying started almost immediately, and Governor Brown vetoed the measure when it reached his desk in April of 1980—though some of the bill's supporters would later argue that he didn't sign the veto quickly enough to keep the bill from becoming law. Under the rules of the Kentucky legislature, any veto from the governor had to be made within ten days of the bill's passage; Governor Brown didn't veto SB 263 until eleven days after it was passed through the house. This issue would continue to come up several years after the bill was presumed dead by most parties when Senator Kelsey Friend, who represented Eastern Kentucky's Pike County, asked the State Attorney General's office to consider whether this bill had, in fact, legalized cockfighting years before.

Whatever his intentions, SB 283 would follow Bailey through his legislative career, with opponents often pointing to it as proof that Bailey was a hillbilly—many of them not understanding that he'd always claimed that label proudly; it was the word's connotation he so ardently objected to. The controversy that surrounded these pieces of legislation wasn't truly about cockfighting; it was about people outside Appalachia constantly casting them in a negative light rather than acknowledging their cultural heritage. It was not funding for the arts to which Bailey objected; it was the idea that people from the hollows needed to be "schooled" or "cultured" that he resisted. He simply thought Appalachian culture should be given the same respect as that of the big cities, and fought to promote the culture of his Eastern Kentucky home in the legislature as he did in his public comments. Unfortunately, his political opponents often exaggerated this very minor aspect of Bailey's work in the Senate, using topics like arts funding or the legalization of cockfighting to paint him with the stereotypical hillbilly brush in an attempt to discredit his attempts at reform.

Education

While Senator Bailey is most proud of his legislation to limit the Broad Form Deed, to bring mental health services to East Kentucky through the Health Care Reform Act of 1990, the establishment of the Osteopathic Medical Scholarship Program and the return of 50% of the Coal Severance Tax to the county of coal production, it must be noted he was very involved in the Kentucky Education Reform Act of 1990. Led by Senator Joe Wright, the Kentucky Legislature completely revamped Kentucky's K-12 education system. Benny Ray was a forceful advocate for the inclusion of human resource funding during this time. As the Secretary of Human Resources stated, "Human resources got a bigger piece of a much bigger pie thanks to Senator Bailey's efforts." The Youth Service Center and Family Resource Center portion of the Kentucky Education Reform Act is quite similar to the ALCOR community center program. The only amendment adopted on the floor of the Senate during the passage of the Kentucky Education Reform

Act was Senator Bailey's amendment moving administration of the Family Resource Centers and Youth Service Centers from the Department of Education to the Cabinet for Human resources.

The Politics of Legislature

In the early 20th century, the Kentucky legislature was by and large controlled by the governor. He would determine who was made the president of the senate and would dictate which legislation would fail and which would pass, even controlling what kinds of bills made it to the senate floor for a vote. Incoming freshman senators would be taken to the governor's office to be told how they were supposed to vote and what they were supposed to do. A group that called themselves "the Black Sheep" challenged this status quo in the 1970s. They opposed the governor's attempts to control the legislative branch, working on their legislation regardless of how he wanted them to vote and laying the groundwork for more democratic separation between the branches of the government. As the 1980 legislative session started, the big question on many people's minds was whether new Governor John Y. Brown, Jr. would continue in this tradition—and if so, whether the Black Sheep would continue their work against him. Bailey fell in with the Black Sheep on his arrival in the senate, appreciating their commitment to making real change for the state rather than serving as a mouthpiece for the executive branch.

As it would turn out, though, Brown had no interest in controlling the legislature the way past governors had. Bailey and his fellow freshman senators were never taken in to the governor's office to be told how they should vote—which was probably for the best, considering it's doubtful they would've gone along with him anyway. Governor Brown saw the trend toward greater independence in the senate and knew he would get burned if he tried to control the legislature the way past governors had. Instead, he used persuasion and compromise to fight for the issues he thought deserved the senate's attention, and accepted their judgment when they disagreed with his policies. The education reform he proposed during the 1980 session was one example. Education reform was one of the primary issues commanding Governor Brown's attention going into the 1980 legislative session but he never tried to make any shady deals behind closed doors to make it pass; he just asked people to support it because he thought it would be good for their districts and the people of the state. The measure ultimately lost by one vote; the way Brown handled both the session and the bill's defeat won him the respect of many legislators, even those who disagreed with his policies.

Benny Ray had the privilege of serving with five Kentucky Governors and witnessed the Kentucky Legislature evolve from a branch of government completely dominated by the Executive Branch to an independent, equal branch of government.

He also formed his own opinions about each Governor he served with. "Governor John Brown, Jr., was the best Governor I served with," Bailey says. "Governor Brown was very self-confident. He knew he was Governor and felt comfortable in having pretty strong people in Cabinet positions. He was excellent in putting together programs that helped people but also protected the financial integrity of the Commonwealth." Bailey was also in the Senate during the term of Governor Martha Layne Collins, the first female Governor of Kentucky. "Governor Collins was excellent in her understanding of the education issues and turned out to be an exceptional economic development leader for Kentucky." Her recruitment of the Toyota factory in Georgetown was a tremendous economic boom to the Commonwealth. Wallace Wilkinson, a businessman with no government experience, didn't really have plans for Kentucky; it seemed he just wanted to be Governor. He was singularly obsessed with the issue of succession. In 1987, when Governor Wilkinson was elected, Kentucky Governors could only serve one term. Trying to change this was Governor Wilkinson's priority but he failed to get it done. He did get a statewide lottery passed and presided over the revamping of Kentucky's educational system through the Kentucky Education Reform Act (KERA), but this was more the result of a Supreme Court ruling demanding that the legislature revamp the entire educational system rather than Governor Wilkinson's interest in education. Benny Ray Bailey says that, in his opinion, Governor Breton Jones "was the best man to serve in the Governor's office while I was in the Senate." Governor Jones had a high interest in the health care issue and worked tirelessly to make affordable health care services available to all Kentuckians. He was successful in this mission, though his victory wouldn't last long.

The system he put into place was systematically weakened and eventually destroyed by succeeding Governors who didn't have the same understanding of and commitment to the issue. Governor Paul Patton was somewhat similar to Governor Wilkinson in that he didn't really have plans he wanted to implement but just wanted to be Governor. Governor Patton, a former coal mine operator, seemed to have a real zeal for limiting coal miners' right to compensation for occupational diseases and was able to pass very restricting programs that denied health care benefits to coal miners. He did pass sweeping higher education programs that, in Bailey's opinion, "improved Kentucky's system of higher education at all levels." When talking about the governors, Benny Ray adds, "I'm quite sure that these Governor's also had, and have, opinions about my service in the Senate. Taken as a whole, these five people that were Governor when I served in the Senate were capable, dedicated and exceptional leaders for Kentucky."

People talk about the partisan nature of the Kentucky state legislature during the late '80s and early '90s as an indication of unrest and division within the House and Senate, but this assessment misses an important aspect of the shift. The legislature had been controlled by the Democratic caucus so consistently the previous few decades that the political process had grown stagnant, with a lot of decisions being made in closed meetings and committees rather than in open debate on the legislative floor. As a representative of an area whose voice had often gone unheard under the old status quo, the loss of ten seats to the Republicans over eight years that shifted some power away from the Democratic majority, Benry Ray saw an opportunity. Even though his policies made him one of the more liberal members of the state Senate, Bailey understood that the republican senators were just looking to get the best possible outcomes for their districts. They disagreed on the issues but could find common ground when it came to taking care of the people of Kentucky. "We're a Commonwealth," Bailey reminded one senator who asked why he should vote on a measure that didn't affect his district. "If it's good for the state I live in, it's good for everybody." Being willing to work across party lines made it easier to find people willing to support his bills when they came to the senate floor.

Even though Bailey believed in transparency in government, he understood the political system well enough to use it to his advantage when the situation called for it. This was especially true of his work as chairman of the Health and Welfare committee. In one particular instance, a bill dealing with HIV and AIDS patients came to the Senate in 1990. The bill itself would provide for AIDS education and training in how to deal with the infection for health care professionals, along with changes to testing procedures and protection for those afflicted by it. The problem came when Senators added amendments to the bill while it was in the Health and Welfare Committee. These amendments greatly weakened the bill, restricting the rights of those suffering from the disease in the guise of protecting the public health. One provision would require doctors to report the names of those infected with the virus, while another required their sexual partners be notified. The more egregious amendments included one that made it a Class D felony for an HIV-positive person to knowingly have sex without obtaining their partner's permission, and another that would allow food service establishments to fire or refuse to hire someone on the basis of their HIV positive status. Bailey quietly removed the amendments and placed the bill on the consent calendar, where it was approved by the senate before anyone noticed the amendments were gone. Six senators protested and changed their votes to a no after the bill was passed, but too late for the act of defiance to go on record; officially, the unamended bill passed the senate with a unanimous 37-0 vote.

As chairman of the Health and Welfare Committee, Bailey remained committed to the open dialogue and bipartisan cooperation he encouraged on the senate floor. Conservative Republican Senator Jack Trevey, who represented an affluent district of Lexington and sat on the Health and Welfare Committee, acknowledged that Senator Bailey was far more liberal than him, but that they nonetheless agreed on many of the public health issues they addressed. Speaking to The State Journal in 1990, Trevey said Bailey was "very fair, up front in the committee, telling us what he's going to do, where he stands." When he opposed proposals in his committee, Bailey would tell the sponsors his stance up front.

Though he was a crafty political operator, comfortable with the behind the scenes work of the political process, he above all supported the democratic process as a way of ensuring all people in the Commonwealth were heard and respected equally. "I've been accused of a whole lot of things," Bailey said. "I've never been accused of not giving people their day in court.

Bailey's ability to reach across the aisle was put to the test when a Supreme Court mandate forced Kentucky to redistrict in the mid-'90s. The ruling said that district lines should divide no more counties than was mathematically possible. As a result, Bailey's 29th District was altered to include Johnson County, an area of the state that traditionally voted Republican. This pitted him up against the county's incumbent Republican senator, John David Preston, in the next general election. Both Bailey and Preston had been popular in their respective districts. Preston considered Bailey's long tenure in the Senate to be a point against him as the election approached, saying, "From what I hear, people are waiting on this election."

The campaign Bailey ran in Johnson County was not so different than those he'd run in more familiar neighboring counties like Knott and Perry. The concerns that Democratic- leaning counties in Eastern Kentucky had were largely shared by Johnson County, and Bailey's established voting record in support of the region was an asset as he began his re- election campaign. He pointed to the fact that he had fought to keep taxes low, fighting to lower taxes 25 times in the past five years and asserting as he had since the beginning that the key was better government, not bigger government. He spoke of the state government's role in providing the region's infrastructure, calling it "the best work government can do" to help the region's economy. The road ways in Eastern Kentucky had improved dramatically since Bailey ran his initial senate campaign in 1979, in large part thanks to his consistent work on the issue. Roads like the Mountain Parkway, Route 15, Route 80, and US 23 were expanded and connected throughout Eastern Kentucky to give all the region's residents access to Class A roads. Bailey announced plans to follow this up with work on renovations to secondary roads in his re-election campaign. His message on jobs and welfare also resonated with Johnson County's residents. For able-bodied citizens, he fought to remove any obstacles to their ability to work for a fair wage; for those who were disabled, he helped build and fund programs to support them.

The support of organizations like Kentucky's AFL CIO, the United Mine Workers of America, and other unions and blue-collar groups certainly helped Senator Bailey's credibility with his new voters in Johnson County, but it was his interaction with them on a face-to-face level that was imperative to winning their votes away from Senator Preston. Bailey spent several days traveling through various parts of Johnson County, speaking with the people to learn their views on the issues and what they wanted out of their government. After his tour of the county, Bailey put an article in their local paper describing his past work and plans for the next legislative session, including projects specific to Johnson County, like improving the tourism potential of Paintsville Lake. Bailey also had the strong support of Republican State Representative Ray Preston and his family. This was a tremendous help in the Republican dominated County. The combination of his strong record in the senate and his on the ground work in the county allowed Bailey to defeat Preston in the November election.

On the state senate level, Senator Bailey was accused of orchestrating a coup in 1997, when long-time Senate President John "Eck" Rose ran for re-election. Five Democratic senators, including Bailey, Walter "Doc" Blevins, Glenn Freeman, Gary Johnson, and Larry Saunders, formed an alliance with the Republican caucus to get Saunders voted in as the new Senate President. Four of the five senators who'd sided with the Republicans represented Mountain districts. Though Bailey denied being the mastermind behind the plot, he acknowledged that he was glad to see a change in the Senate leadership. "Voting blocs are over with in terms of us all going down there in lock-step," Bailey said to reporters, adding, "We can't set a Democratic agenda to the exclusion of the Republicans."

Political commentator David Porter said Eastern Kentucky "should be extremely proud to call Senators Bailey, Blevins, Freeman, and Johnson our Senators" because of what they'd accomplished, which would encourage a more open and democratic legislature and do a great service in the future to the needs of the region. The senators' fellow Democrats were less enthused about the decision. They accused Bailey of ousting Senator Rose out of vengeance—Bailey had lost to Rose in a race for Senate President in 1986. Governor Paul Patton denounced the senators who'd sided with the Republicans; all five were banished from the Democratic caucus and accused of abandoning the party. Senator Rose called Bailey a maverick who didn't know how to support and work with his fellow Democrats. Senator David Karem pointed to the fact that Bailey had remained outside of the senate's power structure for his entire 17-year tenure to that point, calling it a sign of Bailey's inability to cooperate. According to Karem, someone who'd been in the senate that long "should be able to build the confidence and trust of members to such a degree that you do move ahead in the process." Absent from Karem's reasoning was the possibility that Bailey's resistance to the status quo— the same quality that allowed him to bring about reforms—was the reason for his past exclusion from the hierarchy. When asked about the coup, Bailey said, "Senator Rose and Senator Karem were good legislators. Senator Karem was a friend and I enjoyed working with him. Others that I enjoyed a wonderful friendship and working relationship with were Senators Danny Meyer, Georgia Powers, Charles Berger, Art Schmidt, Jack Trevey, Joe Wright, Mike Moloney, Ed O'Daniel, Henry Lackey, John Rogers, Frank Miller, Danny Yocum, Gary Johnson, Walter

Blevins, Glen Freeman, Kelsey Friend, John Doug Hays, Denny Nunnelly, Delbert Murphy, David Boswell, Gus Sheehan, Joe Meyer, Nelson Allen, Lewis Penniston and Charles Borders. [These] were friends that I respected very much and worked with throughout my senate career. The three bills I sponsored that I considered to be of major importance, the Broad Form Deed amendment, the Health Care Reform Act of 1990, and the medical scholarship program in 1 998, passed the Senate and the House without a dissenting vote. This would seem to contradict Karem's assertion that Senator Bailey 'should be able to build the confidence and trust of the members.' I guess the positive or negative aspects of my Senate service would depend on which end of the horse one was talking to. The fact is, there were 29 democratic state senators when Senator Rose was elected President of the Senate in 1987. While the House of Representatives maintained their Democratic majority and three successive gubernatorial races returned Democrats to the Governor's office, Senator Rose saw the Democrats in the state senate dwindle to 20 during his ten-year term. He offered himself as a Democratic candidate for Governor in 1995 and was beaten badly and as a Democratic candidate for Congress in 1998 and lost again. Senator Rose was not very good for the Democratic Party."

One of the problems that had led to the shake-up of the Senate leadership that happened in 1996 was the fact that the party had moved away from its greatest strengths. The Democratic Party in Kentucky had always represented the blue-collar worker. It was the party of the Mine Workers Union, historically advocating on behalf of the disenfranchised against the big businesses that wanted to trample them. Senator Rose's voting record didn't show this kind of support for working class Kentuckians. He'd supported the atrocious 1980 worker compensation legislation and was vocal about his intent to repeal the 1994 Prevailing Wage Restoration Act, tried to repeal the unmined minerals tax which would have been devastating for schools in the coal fields — and was not the only Democratic senator this was true of. For a senator like Benny Ray Bailey who cared more about the principles than the label, working with Republican senators was no different than working with many of his fellow Democrats; he disagreed with both groups on a lot of points, but knew they could find common ground on the issues that would serve both of their districts.

After the coup, Bailey was named the chairman of the Appropriations and Revenue Committee, the most powerful standing committee in the Senate because of its role in overseeing the state budget. He was also named a member of the State and Local Government and Education Committees following the coup.

Bailey wielded the power he'd been given as the chairman of the Senate Appropriations and Revenue Committee with the same single- minded dedication to his district that he'd used in his previous chairman position on the Health and Welfare Committee. Money obtained for the district through the state budget helped to expand the Otter Creek Correctional Center, creating more jobs for Floyd County residents. A new building was constructed at Prestonsburg Community College's Floyd County campus, with a new center for Science, Mathematics, and Technology that would improve the region's access to higher education. Other local colleges, like the Lees College and Hindman extended campuses of Hazard Community College, were given significant funding. Projects to improve the water and sewage systems of major cities in Floyd and Knott Counties were also funded, along with new senior citizen centers in Prestonsburg, Mud Creek. Betsy Layne, McDowell and Wayland, as well as major renovations to senior citizen centers at Wheelwright and Martin. All-told, Bailey was able to bring over $50 million worth of projects and funding to his district through his work on the committee.

In January of 1999, Bailey was again chosen as Times Person of the Year for Knott County because of his work through the committee that brought millions of dollars into the county. In addition to these practical considerations, the paper praised Bailey's leadership throughout his time in the Senate, calling it "a positive reflection on Knott County" and adding that "when one Knott Countian shines in the pinnacle of power in Frankfort, the county and its people share in the respect."

Johnson County also had reason to celebrate once Bailey was named the chairman of the Senate Appropriations and Revenue Committee. The county had been added to Bailey's district thanks to the redistricting of the mid-'90s, a move that initially led to concern within the county that it would be ignored in favor of the counties where Bailey had an established history. Residents of Johnson County were delighted when this turned out not to be the case. In fact, Bailey secured just as much funding for Johnson County through his work as chairman of this influential committee as he did for more long- term counties like Knott and Floyd. The most significant project Bailey was able to obtain funding for was the construction of a campground and other improvements at Paintsville Lake. The lake was located on a state park that had for a long time been the oldest state park to have never received any development projects—in essence, making it a state park in name only. Johnson County had been promised improvements to Paintsville Lake for years by previous representatives; the $2.85 million Bailey was able to obtain for the county was the first time a representative delivered on these promises, proving—as one local reporter put it— that Johnson County "will not be treated like the stepchild of his district." The Paintsville Lake project wasn't the only funding Bailey secured for Johnson County; a $250,000 river walkway along Paint Creek was funded, running from downtown to Mayo Plaza, and $200,000 was given to the rescue squads in Floyd County for new equipment and building renovations. The Johnson County Homeplace Economic Development Program brought another $300,000 of coal severance tax revenues back to the region.

With nearly two decades of work in the state government under his belt, Bailey was no stranger to being called out in the media. He'd weathered past controversies over unpopular legislation, clashes with corporations, and his crafty political plays in previous committee appointments. This most recent drama didn't faze him any more than the previous incidents had. He continued his work in support of his district, not only by securing them a greater share of the state budget but also by improving the lines of communication between Eastern Kentucky and the state legislature in Frankfort.

In the summer of 1998, Bailey organized a series of meetings between state cabinet representatives and local government officials from Eastern Kentucky's counties. Rather than have the county officials come to Frankfort, he had the cabinet representatives go to them, a new approach to bringing the government to the people that let officials ask questions about the progress of projects the state had promised to the regions. This novel approach was well-received by both Bailey's constituents and the political media, but the positive publicity was not enough to prevent the firestorm that was to come.

In the summer of 1999, two of the Senate's Democratic legislators switched parties. This gave the Republicans an unprecedented 20-18 majority in the State Senate—the first time the Republicans had controlled power in the legislature in the state's history. The Republican Caucus called for Larry Saunders to step down as Senate President on the basis that the leadership position should go to someone from the new majority party; they named David Williams their nominee for Senate president. Saunders resisted the take-over, threatening to take the matter to the courts and insisting that he'd been elected to a two-year term and should be allowed to continue in his current post until that time had expired. The Democratic caucus was still upset with Saunders, though, believing now that he had laid the foundation of the Republican takeover of the senate and that it was his mean-spirited treatment of his fellow party members that had led the two senators to defect to the Republican Party; he would get neither help nor sympathy from his fellow party members. On January 4, 2000, Saunders stepped down as Senate President rather than risking a long legal and political struggle that would prevent the legislature from being productive during the upcoming General Assembly.

The Republicans were quick to solidify their power in the Senate after Saunders' resignation. They named members of their party as chairmen of all the standing Senate committees, ending Bailey's control of the Senate Appropriations and Revenue Committee. Even with most of his visible power removed, though, Bailey remained the same keen political operator he'd been his entire time in the senate. Even without any obvious influence, Bailey managed to obtain funding for a new judicial centers in Johnson, Knott, Perry and Breathitt County, along with other money for a new Hindman City Hall and millions for water and sewer projects throughout Senate District 29. Unfortunately for Bailey, and East Kentucky, the loss of his committee seats wouldn't be the only fall-out from the Republican takeover. Coal industry operators, who had long been at odds with Bailey and his many attempts to restrict their continued attempts to take advantage of Eastern Kentucky and its people, saw in the continuing controversy their chance to unseat the popular Senator. Though Bailey had sponsored or supported several pieces of legislation throughout his two decades of service that the coal industry saw as limiting their business, it was specifically an incident from 1996 that had them now gunning for the Hindman Mafia Don. Governor Patton had championed legislation that gutted Kentucky's black lung program, making it much more favorable to the coal operators than the coal workers. Bailey was one of only six senators to stand up to Patton and fight against the weakening of these regulations. This was seen by the coal industry as the last straw; they promised to find someone to run against Bailey that would beat him in the 2000 primary.

Their chosen candidate was a soft- spoken man by the name of Johnny Ray Turner. A newcomer to politics, Turner was best- known as the basketball coach at Johnson County's Central High School—not necessarily the track record and experience that would typically make a candidate stand out in a fight against Bailey, but the combination of the recent attacks on Bailey's credibility and character, the lingering negative feelings from the Senate coup, and the financial backing given to Turner by the coal industry served to make the 2000 primary the toughest political battle Bailey had ever waged.

The coal industry (through Turner) used the coup as the center of its disinformation campaign. Turner's election mailings called Bailey out for his "power play," which he claimed "handed the Senate to the Republicans on a silver platter." Since the Republicans went on to decimate worker's compensation legislation that would have benefitted injured miners in Eastern Kentucky, Turner asserted that Bailey was directly responsible for the alterations made to that legislation. Turner's smear campaign included ads that associated Bailey with Governor Paul Patton—known as a former coal operator whose work in office had been generally unfavorable to the 29th District's largely blue-collar constituents— calling them close friends even though they had never been close, politically or personally. A sound clip from Governor Patton, from an April event in Hazard, had him joking that Perry County "is the only county I've ever seen that's got two senators," alluding to the idea that Bailey was still more concerned with the economic status of Perry County, which had been in his district before the lines were redrawn, than he was with the counties that remained in his district. This claim was contradicted by the millions of dollars in funding Bailey had obtained for Johnson, Breathitt, Knott, and Floyd Counties while he still held the chairmanship of the Appropriations and Revenue Committee; fact is, it has been calculated that if the money Bailey had allocated to his district in 1998 and 2000 were in dollar bills they would reach from East Kentucky to the Pacific Ocean and back, 5 times. No other legislative district in Kentucky received more state funding in 1998 and 2000 than District 29 in East Kentucky. The advertisements put out by Turner twisted the facts to make it seem as if Bailey was neglecting his district in favor of his own interest.

Even as the election was taking place, Bailey questioned the ethics and sources of funding in Turner's campaign. Bailey believed Turner had been recruited to run against him by Ross Harris, a lawyer from Pikeville who had interests in the coal industry. Harris denied these accusations, claiming he was helping Turner only because Bailey "has not represented the four counties in his district," a reasoning consistent with the Turner campaign advertisements but not with Bailey's record in the legislature.

There was no denying that Turner was better funded than Bailey, though exactly how much money Turner used on his campaign was unclear. He admitted to spending $350,000 but the actual figure was probably higher, with financial reports taken for both opponents after the election indicating Turner was likely given money from dubious sources. Though Turner was a first-time politician, his father had also been in politics, and had in fact run against Bailey in the 1983 election; Turner had more connection to the political system than he wanted to admit, presenting himself as an everyman and political outsider.

In the years following the election, information began to surface that showed Bailey's accusations of impropriety in the election were not a simple case of sour grapes. An examination of the campaign's financial records in the early 2000s revealed that Turner had paid 650 different people a total of $34,000 to haul voters, a long- acknowledged way of influencing elections; Turner claimed the payment was for legitimate employment as drivers helping people get to polling places. Charges were levied that Turner wrote blank checks in amounts from $24 to $60, which were then given to "various middlemen who distributed them to voters." Turner had raised an incredible amount of money for a political newcomer, with most of his campaign contributors giving the maximum allowed amount of $1,000, leading to suspicions that many were straw contributors used to funnel money from Harris into Turner's campaign. In 2004, Glenn Turner (John Turner's cousin and a high official in his senate campaign) and Ross Harris were convicted of mail fraud in a Pike County case. In May of 2005, Johnny Turner, Glenn Turner, and Ross Harris were indicted by a federal grand jury for paying people to vote.

Whether it had been his idea or not, however, it was clear that the 2000 election had not been conducted in a fair way, and it was likely that Turner had used similarly unsavory tactics in his following campaigns; in 2004, Turner defeated Eric Hamilton by a narrow 26-vote margin of victory, after 75 absentee votes turned up in Floyd County and Senator Turner received all 75! Senator Turner was still in this second term of the senate when he pled guilty of election fraud in April of 2007 following a lengthy federal investigation. Turner pled guilty to misdemeanor violation of non-willfully making campaign expenditures for the purpose of influencing voters; this plea was part of a deal to make the government drop a felony voter fraud indictment.

Turner was sentenced to three months of home detention followed by one year of probation. U.S. District Judge Karen Caldwell referred to Turner as a "willing victim" during the proceedings, telling him during the sentencing, "In this court's perspective, it has been very lenient in granting no jail time. You had a real brush with disaster here...and it's been narrowly averted." Glenn Turner's sentencing was less lenient, including six months in prison for lying to the federal jury about the source of $1,000 contributions made by his friends and family during the 2002 Pike County judicial race.

Senator Turner continued to serve in the State Senate despite the election fraud charges, winning re-election again in 2008. In his time in the State Senate, Turner has not been the same kind of active advocate Eastern Kentucky had in Benny Ray Bailey. The soft-spoken basketball coach became a relatively quiet senator, sponsoring few bills and making no waves outside of his criminal guilty pleas. The events leading up to Johnny Ray Turner's shocking upset in the 29th District had shifted the power in the state government in favor of the Republican party; the election itself revealed the extent to which corruption had been allowed to fester in the state's political system, not only because of the various criminal convictions and federal investigations but because those convicted of these offenses, like Turner, were allowed to continue in their positions. The combination of a Republican majority with members of state government who clearly represented coal industry interests was especially worrying considering the legislators elected in November would be responsible for legislative redistricting that would establish the state's politically boundaries for the next ten years.

During Benny Ray Bailey's time in the Kentucky State Senate, much was accomplished for his East Kentucky senate district and for the entire East Kentucky region. While Senator Bailey never claimed sole credit for any improvement, he was there each day working for his constituents and is given all or partial credit for many improvements.

Included in these improvements are:

- Raising the average teacher pay from $7500 in 1980 to over $35,000 in 2000.
- Full funding of the Teachers' Retirement System and the Kentucky Employees Retirement system each year from 1980-2000.
- Legislation that returned 50% of coal severance tax to coal producing counties.
- New Route 680 to connect Route 80 at Garrett to US 23 at Harold.
- Improvements to Route 205 in Breathitt County.
- Re-construction of Kentucky Route 3 from Prestonsburg to Inez.
- Over $3 million in grants for improvements to school facilities in the Johnson County Public School system. Over $800,000 in grants for improvements to the Paintsville Independent School System.
- The Dry Creek Bridge replacement bridge and turning lanes.

- The new intersection at Route 899 and Route 17, Mouth of Caney.
- Improvements of Route 899, the Alice Lloyd College bypass, the lowering of the grade across Caney Mountain, and improvements to the intersection of KY Route 899 and Route 160.
- Three new bridges in Hindman. The new Hindman City Hall.
- The Hindman Branch of Hazard Community and Technical College.
- Three new buildings at Hazard Community and Technical College.
- Three new buildings at Prestonsburg Community and Technical and the Science and Math Building at Prestonsburg Community College.
- New Regional Hospital in Perry County.
- The Regional Psychiatric Hospital, only mental hospital east of Lexington.
- The UK Center of Excellence in Rural Health Building. UK educational programs for physician residency, medical technology, nursing and physical therapy located in East Kentucky.
- New Senior Citizens Centers in Wayland, McDowell, Mud Creek, Betsy Layne and Prestonsburg. Major renovations to Senior Citizens Centers in Martin and Wheelwright.
- New equipment, including big screen TV's and computers, for Senior Citizens Centers for Jackson, Hazard, Hindman and Paintsville.
- First improvements, including campgrounds and marina, in the history of Paintsville Lake State Park.

- New convention center and marina at Buckhorn State Park.
- Improvements to Route 122 at Hite, Hi Hat, Buckingham. South Floyd High School Building.
- South Floyd High School Recreation Area and Football Field.
- Prestonsburg High School Recreation Area and Football Field.
- New Duff Elementary School.
- New May Valley Elementary School. New Allen Elementary School.
- New Gymnasiums at MC Napier, Dilce Combs, Buckhorn High Schools.
- New Gymnasium for Jackson City Schools.
- New Football Stadium at Breathitt County High School. New Baseball Stadium at Knott County Central High School.
- New lights for football fields at Knott County Central, Allen Central and Betsy Layne High Schools.
- New lights for Cordia High School Baseball Field.
- New Justice Centers for Breathitt County, Knott County, Perry County, Floyd County and Johnson County.
- Improvements on Route 160 at Knott County Central High School.
- Addition to jobs at Wheelwright Prison, 1998. Improvements to Wheelwright Sewer System. Drinking Water Treatment Plant for Floyd County. Improvements to Johnson County Library.
- Caney Creek Rehabilitation Center.

- Crisis Intervention Center in Breathitt County. Improvements to drainage system in the City of Prestonsburg.
- Expanding Medicaid for Pregnant Women and Children to age 1 to 185% of Poverty Income Level.
- Swing bed conversion for small hospitals, i.e., McDowell ARH.
- Free Hospital treatment for all persons with incomes up to 100% of poverty level.
- New water treatment plant on Carr Fork Lake for Knott County.
- New water lines for Knott, Floyd, Breathitt and Johnson Counties.
- Money for Lees College to transition to the Hazard Community and Technical College program.
- Removal of the last tolls from the Mountain Parkway.
- The UK Center for Rural Health Building in Hazard, now called the "Bailey-Stumbo Building."
- Scholarships for all Kentucky residents to attend the Pikeville Medical School.
- Summer program for prospective medical students from East Kentucky at Pikeville Medical School.

CHAPTER EIGHT

NIKKI DEREATH RIECK BAILEY

No story of the life of Benny Ray Bailey could be complete without the story of the life of Nikki Rieck Bailey and vice versa. Nikki came into Benny Ray's life in 1971 and changed his life forever. The following pages depict a short history of her life and is meant as a memoir for her family.

Nikki Dereath Rieck was born on March 8, 1950 to Chester (Chet) Robert Rieck and Vera Lee Rieck in Lewellen, Nebraska. Nikki was the third child in the family of four children. She had one sister, Suzanne (Sue), born in 1948, and two brothers, Byron (Barney) born in 1946 and Danny, born in 1955. Nikki's maternal grandfather emigrated from Norway but abandoned the family in the late 1920s and the family never knew what happened to him.

Chet and Vera were World War II veterans; Chet served in the Pacific War Theater and Vera in the European theater. Vera, as a registered nurse, was in the Army while Chet served in the Marines. Vera rose to the rank of Lieutenant before being discharged. She was featured in the books War Letters and Angels of Mercy. Vera was also featured on ABC's "Good Morning America" in 2001. Chet served with distinction and was awarded several medals for bravery for his service.

Lewellen, Nebraska, home to the Rieck family, is in Western Nebraska and is a very small town, population less than 200. It is located in Garden County, along the Oregon Trail. The primary vocation is farming and Nikki's family was part of the farming community. Nikki's early years were spent on her paternal grandfather's farm with her parents and siblings. Her grandparents passed in the 1950's and the family moved from Lewellen to another small town, Brule. Nikki's dad continued to farm while Vera worked as a RN in the local hospital. Nikki began Kindergarten in Lewellen but went to West Vail in Brule for the first through third grade.

Nikki's dad often lamented that all the farm income was going to John Deere, to pay for equipment, and to Gulf Oil, to pay for gasoline to operate the equipment. Chet had tried his hand at gold prospecting in Alaska and long haul trucking prior to his marriage but was always drawn back to the farm. Chet was a successful farmer; he won the award for producing the most corn per acre in Nebraska. However, the family farm was a dying operation in the 1950's and Chet saw that he just couldn't raise his family with farm income.

In the late 1950s, Chet's friend, Dick Wlaschin, while visiting the family, asked Chet if he would join him in St. Paul, MN, working for American Hoist. In the early 1960s, Chet accepted a factory job and moved his family to North St. Paul.

Nikki recalls the transition from farm life to city life for the children. "We would run to the corner store without shoes and without coats to buy soda pop and candy. The neighbors looked at us in amazement as those farm kids who couldn't adjust to the 'big city.'" Having lived their life on the farm, city life didn't agree with Chet and Vera, so they began to look for a place to live outside city limits. In 1961, they found a house with 20 acres and a working poultry farm in the village of Wyoming, about 35 miles north of St. Paul. Vera secured a job at a hospital in an adjoining county. She later became Director of Nursing at this hospital, and Chet continued working at American Hoist while running the poultry operation at the Sand Burr Poultry Ranch.

At American Hoist, a new product called fiberglass was being introduced but not embraced by the corporation. American Hoist actually built an addition to their factory to house the fiberglass operation and Chet became the chief worker in this operation. At the same time, Chet began delivering eggs from his "chicken farm" to restaurants and hotels in the Minneapolis and St. Paul area. Nikki recalls getting to ride with her dad to deliver eggs as a young girl. She was amazed that everyone seemed so glad to see her dad when he delivered the eggs and later, thought that the waitresses were "flirting" with her dad.

As Chet sensed the executives at American Hoist were not committed to developing the fiberglass product, he saw an opportunity. He went to the executives and asked if they would give him a contract to furnish the fiberglass chain guards to the corporation. They agreed. Chet became a pioneer in "outsourcing." With a production contract in hand, Chet transitioned his "chicken coops" to a fiberglass factory and began making fiberglass chain guards for American Hoist. He also began making specialty fiberglass products ranging from canoes to historical statues for the villages around Wyoming.

Nikki began school in Wyoming and started to make friends with the other children. She was a typical young girl with the same habits and concerns as all young girls. Nikki attended the Lutheran Church and was confirmed in 1964.

After finishing elementary school, Nikki attended and graduated from Chisago City High School. She was involved in the drama productions and many other school activities.

Outside school, Nikki liked horseback riding, canoeing, camping with her family, and hanging out at the "HUB," a local drive in theater. She was friends with the neighbor Berry children, Susan Mackey and her close childhood friend, Pat Isaac. In 1966, she got her automobile drivers' license and in 1969, got her very first personal car. Now, she was "free" and began to explore Minnesota and, especially, neighboring Wisconsin.

After graduating from high school, Nikki was not very focused on a career but decided to attend Moorhead State University in Moorhead, MN, primarily because some of her friends, most notably Renee Olson and Pat Isaac, were also attending that school. She attended Moorhead for one year but wasn't very happy there.

177

After her year at Moorhead, Nikki returned to Wyoming and, through one of her neighbors, Mark Struble, found employment in Minneapolis with the Honeywell Corporation. She continued to live with her parents and drove the 40 or so miles to Minneapolis each day. Since she had a Blue 1964 Chevy Super Sport, the drive was not too boring!

As she drove to and from the Honeywell job, she thought about her future. She greatly admired her mother and decided she should pursue a career as a registered nurse. She applied for and was accepted to the Arthur B. Anchor School of Nursing in St. Paul. This time, Nikki was focused and knew what she wanted to do. She excelled in the nurse training program.

In the spring of 1971, while reading one of her mother's nursing magazine, Nikki came across an advertisement for summer jobs in rural America for nursing students. The programs were administered by the Student American Medical Association and one of the programs was in Appalachian Kentucky.

Nikki and a few of her nursing school classmates applied for and were accepted for jobs in the summer program. Karen Maurer, Brenda Tiegs, and Pat Reager joined Nikki for the trip to Kentucky in June, 1971. The drive to Kentucky was quite an experience for these flat land city girls. One of the girls' parents belonged to AAA and asked AAA for a map to get to Alice Lloyd College in Pippa Passes, KY, where the summer program was headquartered. AAA responded with directions to within 100 miles of Pippa

Passes and said, from that point, "you are on your own."

They did stop and ask directions but no one knew where the place they were seeking was located. Finally, after driving for many hours, they stopped again and asked directions. The fellow they asked how to get to Alice Lloyd College said, "Ma'am, you're right in the middle of that campus."

The Director of the summer program, called ALCOR, was Benny Ray Bailey; the Director of the Medical portion of the program was Grady Stumbo. There were six colleges in the ALCOR program. Nikki was assigned to work out of Union College in Barbourville, KY; Karen Maurer was assigned to work out of Alice Lloyd College; Brenda Tiegs was assigned to work out of Hazard Community College and Pat Reager was assigned to work out of Cumberland College. The friends from Minnesota were able to get together every four weeks at meetings for the program but lived the summer in their assigned communities.

After the summer of 1971, Nikki returned to Minnesota to finish her nursing education. Again, she excelled in the program and finished the second year of the three-year program in June, 1972 but in the meantime, something happened that changed her life forever.

In November, 1971, Benny Ray Bailey showed up in Minnesota, called Nikki, and they began a long distance romance that lasted through that year. Benny Ray had left the ALCOR program to attend Ohio University to get a Ph.D. and lived in Athens, Ohio. Benny and Nikki's long dis-

179

tance romance was helped by the fact that round trip airline tickets for students from Minneapolis to Columbus, Ohio, were $51. The airlines got quite a business from these two during 1971-1972.

Benny Ray shared with Nikki the hopes and dreams he and Grady Stumbo had to build a nationwide model health care delivery system in Appalachia. In the summer of 1972, Nikki decided she wanted to be part of that dream so she joined Benny Ray, Grady and another alumnus of ALCOR, Glenna Davenport, in Kentucky to pursue this dream. At the beginning, the group had no money, not even a place to live. But that was about to change.

With Nikki, Grady and Glenna taking care of patients at an outpatient clinic at Our Lady of the Way Hospital in Martin, KY, and Benny Ray traveling to New York, Chicago and other places soliciting funds, the clinic building rapidly took shape. In December, 1972, this unlikely group opened the first clinical facility in the history of Knott County, Kentucky. The clinic was complete with a medical laboratory, radiology facilities, a pharmacy, a dental suite and appropriate medical offices.

Something else happened to Nikki that changed her life. In 1973, she and Benny Ray were married. Actually, they left work one morning, went to Virginia, got married and were back to work by noon! Benny Ray has always maintained that Nikki was the prettiest, most compassionate, caring and intelligent person he had ever met.

Today, Benny Ray says, "Nikki has been a wonderful wife, an outstanding mother to our children and a blessing to everyone she meets."

Nikki continued to work in the clinic until the arrival of the couple's first child, Benny Ray II, in 1974. Later, Chet arrived in 1978; Rebekah Dereath, who died at birth, in 1980, and Steven Paul, in 1982. Also, in 1978, Malcolm Glenn decided to come live with Benny and Nikki. Nikki stayed at home to care for the children while they were infants.

In 1979, Benny Ray ran for Kentucky State Senator. Nikki, as she always has, was right there alongside him. Folks tell of meeting Nikki along the dirt roads of Knott, Floyd, Martin and Perry Counties, leading one child and carrying another on her hip, knocking on people's doors asking them to vote for Benny Ray. Benny Ray won the election and went on to serve 21 years in the Kentucky State Senate.

In 1984, with Steven in daycare, Nikki enrolled at Alice Lloyd College to pursue a degree in elementary education—the same Alice Lloyd College she had trouble finding some 13 years earlier. She completed her degree in 1988 and found the degree to be invaluable in helping the children with their schoolwork during their school years.

In 1991, Nikki became a grandmother when Malcolm Glenn had a daughter, Courtney Nicole. While Courtney and her family lived some distance away, Nikki always managed to see her and check on her well-being.

Courtney's annual summer visits were always fun packed and usually included Vacation Bible

School at Big Branch Baptist Church. Courtney was always such a delightful girl.

In 1999, Nikki became a grandmother for the second time with the birth of Benny Ray II daughter, Kennedy. Since Kennedy lived close, Nikki spent a great deal of time with her and constantly encouraged Kennedy to participate in a variety of activities. Horseback riding camps, piano camps, dulcimer camps, bicycle trips and, of course, religious retreats at Camp Nathanael became the norm for summer time for Kennedy and Nikki. For her part, Kennedy responded with enthusiasm. Kennedy joined every club available drama productions, community play productions, singing groups; everything she could get into, she did. Kennedy was always up for a new experience and her "Nana" was right there with her, through her summer at Exeter Academy in New Hampshire in 2012, through her years at Chatham Hall School for Girls in 2013-2015, through her summer at Murray State University in the Governor's Scholars Program in 2016.

In 2006, Nikki's first grandson, Wyatt Benjamin was born to Benny Ray II and his wife Shelly. Wyatt was a handful of joy from the time of his birth. Nana always had time to play with him and offer him new experiences. Wyatt was an extremely intelligent, active and curious child and a real joy to all in the family.

In 2013, another granddaughter, born to Chet, arrived. Kashlynn Monroe was such a beautiful and well behaved young lady. She was content with her Nana, even spending nights and weekends with Nana at a very early age with no problem. She and Nana have developed a strong relationship which only gets better as she grows.

The next grandchild, Emmett Morrison Bailey, was born to Steven and his wife, Lauren, in 2015. While Emmett is still an infant as this is being written, he is such a good baby and a real joy to be around. He never cries, is always in a good mood and really enjoys being the center of everyone's attention.

As she did throughout her life, Nikki relishes being a grandmother and devoted most of her time to this most important aspect of her life. People say that Nikki would crawl through a mile of broken glass to see one of her grandchildren jump rope or play marbles.

After the children were all in school, Nikki returned to work at the clinic but this time, she chose to assist Benny Ray in administration. She took charge of the finances of the clinic and made sure all bills were paid, all staff were paid, that sufficient monies were available to pay for everything and the financial aspects of the clinic were in order. She worked at the clinic for 35 years and she and Benny Ray retired in December, 2015.

The story of the life of Nikki Dereath Rieck serves as an inspiration to all who knew her. She is completely dedicated to her God, her husband, her children and her grandchildren. Her love of family, from her parents to her in laws is legendary among those who know her. Nikki is an example of the life of an American woman in the 21st Century. She prepared herself in every way to be a mother, a provider, and a servant. She is a prime example of the balancing act of working and running a household that all women are faced with. She is today, and has always been, a family person. Nikki talks of her family with great love and appreciation.

"My mother and dad, Chet and Vera Rieck, were exceptional parents. My dad, while he certainly didn't agree with all my decisions and all that I did, always supported me and made sure I knew that he loved me. Dad was one of the most intelligent persons I ever met and such a good provider for his family, both with material things and with the love, direction and advice that made him a great Dad.

"My mother taught me about life and about how to live. Mother was always there for me and for my siblings. She came to Kentucky each time one of my children was born and stayed with us for weeks to help until I could get going again. Mother had advice for me at every stage of my life and, while I didn't always follow her advice, I would have been a better person if I had.

"My mother in law, Viola Bailey, was such a help and inspiration to me. She was always there to help and was invaluable to my family when the boys were growing up. Their Mamaw always bought them gifts on her mostly weekly trips to visit, took them to her house for many overnights, and taught them how to chop wood, climb trees, and make a makeshift light out of cooking oil and old rags when the electricity went out.

"Viola would go shopping and buy 50 pound sacks of onions and potatoes because they were "bargains," and always brought us half. She always had an opinion and would always give it to you if you asked, or if you didn't ask. She was such a help and joy to us.

"My children were wonderful. Ben was such an energetic baby and maintained that exuberance throughout his life. Never embarrassed, never afraid to get in front of a crowd and perform. He also never lacked self- confidence and pursued every hobby from flying airplanes to playing a guitar with solid determination. Ben was compassionate, intelligent and grew into a fine man and wonderful father.

"Chet was always the studious one. He was very serious minded from an early age and excelled in his school work. Chet set about doing things with a plan and always made the plan work. He was serious about his pursuits and enjoyed success in his many endeavors. Chet liked to travel and he liked his Mom and Dad to join him. He really widened our world. Like Ben, he grew to be a wonderful father and is so concerned with the well-being of his fellow man.

"Rebekah Dereath died seconds after she was born. Benny and I have often discussed what she would have been and what she would have meant to our life had she lived. We are confident in where she is and that we will be reunited someday.

"Glenn came to live with us when he was 14 years old. Glenn was very good in sports and excelled in football in high school. He was very intelligent, had a wonderful sense of humor, and was a true joy to our family and to everyone he met. As an adult, he was completely devoted to his daughter, Courtney.

"Steven was the comedian of the family and was such as joy as a child. Steven could laugh at everything and everyone and also, was not afraid to laugh at himself. He was a very good student and excelled in sports especially baseball in high school. Steven was very compassionate and loved everything about living in a rural environment. He worked hard in school, had many friends, and, like Ben and Chet, has grown into a wonderful father."

Nikki feels deeply about family and that no story of her life can be complete without the acknowledgment of the joy her brothers, sister, sisters in law, brothers in law and daughters in law have brought to her life.

"Byron and his wife Karen were always there to greet us and make us feel welcome on our many trips to Minnesota; Danny and his wife Colleen visited us, kept in touch, even made us the Godparents of both their children; Sue and her husband Gary were with us on so many trips to so many places and each time a blessing to be around. Benny's brothers and sisters, Doug and Ann, Emogene and Delmond, Curt and Aileen, and Shannon and Sandy were so good to me and made me feel welcome in their family."

According to Nikki, "Family has always meant a great deal to me and, along with my Mom and Dad, all my family has always been my fulfillment and my inspiration."

About her daughter in laws, Nikki says, "Courtney's mom Susan is such a sweetheart. She is a superb mother to Courtney and has been with Courtney through thick and thin.

Ben's wife Shelly is such a joy and such a blessing to our family and to Ben. She has always been there for all of us whenever we had a need and is a wonderful mother to my grandchildren and she will always have our appreciation and our love. Steven's wife Lauren has been such a blessing to Steven and to me and Benny Ray. She encourages Steven and assists him in all his work. Now, she is proven to be an exceptional mother to our grandson and we love her very much."

Nikki Dereath Rieck Bailey: from the corn fields of Nebraska to the wheat fields of Minnesota to the coal fields of East Kentucky, a remarkable journey for this remarkable lady. Nikki has touched the lives and made a positive difference in the lives of so many. She has been a supporting wife, a loving mother, a servant of her God and a blessing to all she met. She wrote this short history for her family, her children and grandchildren so that they might know a little of her life.

CHAPTER NINE

POST POLITICAL YEARS

If there is one take-away from Benny Ray Bailey's career—not just in the senate, but in his prior work with both ALCOR and the Knott County Clinic—it is his desire to bring positive change to Eastern Kentucky's mountain counties. In the senate, he worked to reform the coal industry, repair long-neglected roadways, introduce new jobs, and improve education, introducing and supporting reforms to improve nearly every aspect of the region. In no area was he more committed than that of rural health care, continuing to run the Knott County Clinic while working in the legislature, as well as authoring and supporting legislation to revolutionize the way health care was delivered to Kentucky's impoverished, rural, and working class citizens. Bailey had been thoroughly committed to Eastern Kentucky well before he joined the senate, and his commitment didn't wane when his senate tenure was over.

In the years after Benny Ray retired from the senate, his focus shifted back to rural—and specifically Appalachian—health care. He still ran the East Kentucky Health Services Center, the clinic in Hindman he'd founded with Dr. Grady Stumbo and his wife Nikki back in 1972. He also had a newer venture in Southern Medical Partners, a recruitment program he'd founded in 1998, to address the problem of how to entice more physicians to practice medicine in the area. Bailey had worked to address this issue many times during his two decades in the senate, including a section devoted to recruitment of talent in his 1990 Health Care Reform Act.

Southern Medical Partners was another means of addressing hospital staffing issues in Eastern Kentucky. The program brought ER doctors in to work full time in the region's five hospitals (in Hazard, Whitesburg, West Liberty, Hyden, and McDowell). In total, this meant around 300 12-hour shifts that had to be filled each month, not even counting the substitute staff Southern Medical Partners sent to other hospitals on request. The organization filled an important need, helping to solve the staffing problems Eastern Kentucky's hospitals had been grappling with to one degree or another for several decades. These issues had in the past meant the region's doctors were overworked and unable to devote sufficient time to their patients; it had also translated to long waits to see a doctor in rural and poor areas, limiting the access many had to necessary services. Southern Medical Partners helped to make sure every hospital had sufficient doctors to treat their region's patients. Bailey ran Southern Medical Partners until he sold the contracts in 2009. He didn't completely step back from rural health care at this point, however; in the early 2010s he served on the Rural Health Oversight Committee, part of the Foundation for a Healthy Kentucky that aimed to continue bring innovative, quality health care to rural areas.

In August 2004, The University of Kentucky opened the Bailey-Stumbo Building in Hazard. The four-story, $13.1 million structure was built with a combination of state, federal, and University funding, some of which Bailey had helped to secure during his time in the senate. The building would serve as the home for health care professional education programs from both the University of Kentucky Center for Rural Health and the Hazard Community and Technical College. Along with classroom and lab space, the building featured outpatient family practice and dental clinics and spaces for community programs, making it a comprehensive health care facility. The building was named for Benny Ray Bailey and Dr. Grady Stumbo to recognize their contributions to Kentucky health care.

Starting from $53 and a dream back in 1972, the duo completely revolutionized the way primary care was provided to rural populations. Their clinic not only provided Appalachian Kentucky with vastly better health care services than it had ever seen in the past, it served as a model for rural health care across the country; many of the most heralded provisions of Bailey's 1990 Health Care Reform were ideas that had come out of his work with the Hindman Clinic. With its emphasis on education and community outreach, the Bailey- Stumbo Building is a shining example of what they worked for so long to achieve.

After leaving the senate in 2000, Benny Ray returned to his work at the clinic. As a young man, Bailey had come back to eastern Kentucky at a time when many instead chose to move away. He encouraged his children to follow that example—not to move out of state in search of greener pastures but to bring their talents back to the Homeplace and make it better. Benny Ray's sons took this message to heart, all of them starting careers in Kentucky. His oldest son, Malcolm Glen, owned and operated a pizza restaurant until he passed away in 2001. Chet also went into the restaurant business in the city and now owns a restaurant. Benny Ray Jr. stayed in his home county, working at the Knott County Clinic and later running it. Steven, the youngest son, became an attorney in an adjoining county. "It's a wonderful place to live if you've got a way to make a living," Bailey says of Eastern Kentucky. When he was in the senate, Benny Ray worked to make sure more people could find that living outside of the coal industry—to make his Homeplace a wonderful place for more people to live.

Despite all the work Benny Ray Bailey and the other Mountain legislators did to bring more resources and services to Eastern Kentucky, it's a slow process making changes to an entire region's economy, especially one that has been so long dependent on a single industry. The region is still reliant on income from the coal industry, which Benny Ray Bailey describes as a yo-yo, saying, "Sometimes you do good, sometimes you don't." While production numbers from Western Kentucky have been slowly dropping over the last decade, the Eastern Kentucky coalfield has seen a dramatic decline in production since

2000. In 2015, the production dropped to its lowest levels since 1932, when the Great Depression slowed industry across the country. Over a quarter of the remaining coal jobs were lost between 2014 and 2015, with a 29% drop in the number of coal industry jobs available in Eastern Kentucky alone. As late as the 2000s, the coal industry was the main source of employment for over 14,000 people in the region; by 2015, it employed only 5,897. There are many reasons for this decline in coal industry employment, but a major factor is the lack of vision on the part of our elected state leaders. Many of these former coal workers had been in the industry their entire lives. With the jobs gone, many of these workers are being forced to look elsewhere, often to the state's Western Coalfield, but there are too many without work and too few jobs for them to fill. Unemployment and underemployment continue to plague the Appalachian populations despite the best efforts of those who have championed them.

Though the individual miners are bearing the brunt of the pain, the county governments of Eastern Kentucky have been hit hard by the industry's recent decline, as well. Many of the services the counties offer are paid for through coal severance tax money. Without that revenue coming in, many of these counties have been forced to limit or even cut services. In other areas, they've been forced to raise taxes on certain services in order to generate enough income to keep everything running. The cumulative effect on the region's people has been devastating, with the very people who need the services of the county the most— those who have recently become un-employed— often living in the same regions that have to cut back the amount of services they offer. The economic situation in Eastern Kentucky is at an overall low point and in desperate need of revitalization.

Bailey continues to work in every way he can to improve the lives of the people of Eastern Kentucky. In addition to his ongoing work with the Knott County Clinic, Benny Ray and Nikki have endowed scholarships at universities in the region to help local students continue their education. Beginning in 2000, Benny Ray and Nikki have established scholarships in every public high school in Floyd and Knott Counties, the county where Benny Ray was born and where he and Nikki have resided. Scholarships at the University of Pikeville are awarded to students from South Floyd and Knott County Central High School; Cordia High School administers its own Benny Ray and Nikki Bailey Scholarship; Big Sandy Community and Technical College has scholarships for students from Betsy Layne, Prestonsburg, and Allen Central High School; and Hazard Community and Technical College awards a scholarship to a Knott County Central High School student each year. In addition, Benny Ray and Nikki created the Benny Ray and Nikki Bailey Foundation which makes periodic cash awards to community and civic groups in Eastern Kentucky to assist in building better communities and improving the chances the children have for their lives. Benny Ray has always advocated students staying in Kentucky to attend college and start careers. If anyone ever doubts whether one or two dedicated young minds can really effect major change in an area, Benny Ray Bailey and Grady Stumbo stand as living examples of how the few can bring about positive change for the many.

At the height of his career, when Bailey held a seat in the State Senate and worked at the Knott County Clinic, he says, "I would wake up sometimes and not know where I was." He lived in Lexington while the Senate was in session, working twelve hour days to bring the best possible outcomes to his district. Even when he lived across the state, though, he stayed connected to his friends and family. He says, "I would still ask Nikki, 'What would this bill really do for the people I represent?'" This question was always foremost on his mind. He raised over $1 million and worked for Dr. Grady Stumbo's run for governor because he believed it would be the best thing for his region. Though they lost, Bailey says, "We ran as good as we could with what we had," competing as they were against candidates with $8 or $9 million bankrolls. Even while he was running the clinic and working as a Senator, Bailey found the time to run both of Stumbo's gubernatorial campaigns, proving himself a man who was never too busy to work for the common good. Representing Eastern Kentucky in the legislature inevitably put Bailey in the position of championing the underdog and the working man, a role he relished. He was never one to back down from a fight when it came to the things he believed in. He was willing to do whatever it took to get Eastern Kentucky the respect and government attention it deserved.

Benny Ray Bailey is the epitome of the self-made man. He was the first one in his family to graduate college, much less earn higher degrees; he used that education to create new opportunities, not only for himself but for other aspiring minds in his region. He has since been recognized with awards and honorary doctorates from his Alma matters for his contributions to society. Every job Bailey had between the year he spent teaching and his seat in the State Senate was one that he created. Benny Ray knew that the jobs he wanted to hold didn't exist yet in his home county—but he also knew that they should exist, and that he was the right person to do them. He had an incredible ability throughout his life to identify the needs of his community and create groups that would fulfill those needs, as he did with the ALCOR program and again with the clinic in Knott County.

Though he was at times a controversial figure in the State Senate, Benny Ray Bailey has left behind a legacy of putting his district's people ahead of personal gain. Regardless of whether or not they agreed with his policies, his fellow senators respected Bailey's commitment to positive change. His willingness to reach across the aisle and cooperate with those who held different views than his own helped to make him one of the most influential state legislators in Eastern Kentucky history. His knowledge of the health care industry was unparalleled, allowing him to make lasting reforms to an industry too complex for many legislators to effectively regulate. He used his positions as chairman of the Health and Welfare Committee—and, later, the Revenue and Appropriations Committee—to secure greater portions of the state budget for Eastern Kentucky's coal counties and bring the region the necessary services it had so long been lacking. Aside from his work in the senate, Bailey's intelligence and integrity challenged popular stereotypes about Appalachian people. His presence in the senate and contributions to society were a stark contrast to the perception of the uneducated backwoods Hillbilly. He proved that people from Eastern Kentucky were just as capable as those from the big city. As he would say, right is right no matter where you come from. He believed the working class deserved a fairer shake—and devoted his life to making sure they got one.

Appendix

Curriculum Vitae

Name Benny Ray Bailey, Ph.D.
Birth date: November 16, 1944
Address: PO Box 849 Hindman, KY 41822
Marital Status Married to Nikki Rieck Bailey,
4 sons, 1 daughter.

Education

Ohio University
Doctoral of Philosophy

University of Michigan School of Public Health

Morehead University
Graduate Work in Administration

Indiana State University
Master of Science

Pikeville College
Bachelor of Arts

McDowell Consolidated School Floyd County,
KY High School Diploma

Work Experience:

Service Station Attendant
1958-1962

Gas Line Maintenance
Summer 1964

Laborer, Hi Hat Elkhorn Mining Company
Summers, 1960 & 1961

Laborer, Taylor Gaskin Steel Mill
Summer 1964

Youth Leadership Development LKLP
Community Action Council Summer, 1966

Teacher, Floyd County Public Schools
1966-1967

Director, Youth Leadership Development LKLP
Community Action Council
Summer, 1967

Assistant Dean of Students Alice Lloyd College
1968-1969

Director of Community Services
Alice Lloyd College
1969-1970

Director of Outreach Programs
Alice Lloyd College
1969-1971

Vice President-Operations ALCOR, Inc.
1969 – 1971

Graduate Assistant Ohio University
1971-1972

Executive Director
East Kentucky Health Services Center, Inc.
1972 – 2015

Kentucky State Senator
1980-2000

Managing Partner
Southern Medical Partners LLC
1998- 2009

Honors and Recognitions

Honorary Doctorate
Pikeville College School of Osteopathic
Medicine 2012

Honorary Doctorate Ohio University
1999

Honorary Doctorate Pikeville College
1998

National Fellowship Award
Indiana State University
1967

Outstanding Young Man of America
1968, 1969, 1970, 1973, 1975, 1976
Community Leaders of America
1970

Academic Scholarship Ohio University
1970

Outstanding Educator of the South
1970

Outstanding Educational Achievement Western Electric Fund
1971

Who's Who in Health Care
1976

John D. Rockefeller III Public Service Award
Woodrow Wilson School Princeton University
1978

Kentucky Association of Health Care Facilities
1990

Area Health Education Center, Hazard
1990

Kentucky Mental Health Association
1991

Carl D. Perkins Service Award
Kentucky Association of Retarded Citizens
1991

Man of the Year Troublesome Creek Times
Knott County Newspaper
1990 & 1998

Leadership Award
East Kentucky Leadership Conference
1991

Number 1 Legislator,
1968-1988
Kentucky River Area Development District
1988

Leadership Award
Kentucky Business and Professional Women
1990

Kentucky Sheriffs Association Leadership
Award
1988

Appreciation Award
Dilce Combs High School Alumni Association
1986

Executive Director s Award
Kentucky River Area Development District
1982

Chairman: Human Services Committee
Southern Legislative Conference
1992, 1993, 1994, 1995

Chairman and Founder
Ky. Primary Care Association

1977-1979

State Senator
29th Kentucky Senate District
1980- 2000

Alumni Medal of Merit
Ohio University Alumni Association
1979

Outstanding Freshman Senator
Capitol Press Corps
1980 Legislative Session

Distinguished Alumni Award
Indiana State University
1980

Chairman
KY River Area Development District
1982- 1983

Chairman
KY State Senate Committee on Health and
Welfare 1984-1996

Chairman
KY State Senate
Budget Sub-committee on Health and Welfare
1982-1996

Chairman
KY State Senate
Appropriations and Revenue Committee
Kentucky Welfare Reform Coalition
1997-1999

Kentucky Hospital Association Award
1990

Papers Presented

"Youth Looks at the Bicentennial" and
Speeches American Revolution Bicentennial
Administration Washington, D.C.
1971

"Student Outreach Programs - Are They Working?"   American Association of Higher Education Chicago, IL
1971

"Student Activism in the 70's" The Conference
Board   New York, NY
1971

"Community Utilization of Volunteers" University Year for Action Conference National Press
Club Washington, D.C.
1972

"America's Third Century" Panel for Century
Three San Francisco, CA
1973

"Rural Manpower Needs"
Innovative Uses for America's Manpower
Conference Battelle Research Center
Seattle, WA
1974

"The Use of Physician Extenders" Kentucky
General Assembly Committee on Health
Frankfort, KY
1974

"The Hope for a Meaningful Bicentennial"
United States Senate Committee on the Arts
Washington, D.C.
1976

"Development and Administration of Primary
Care" and Speeches A Conference on Primary
Care Frontier Nursin Service
Hyden, KY
1976

"Planning and Development of Primary Health
Care" American Association for
Comprehensive Health Planning
New Orleans, LA
1976

"Rural Primary Care"
Georgia Department for Human Resources St.
Simons Island, GA
1979

"Health Care in Transition"
U.K. Medical School Faculty
1988

"Kentucky's Rural Health Care Legislation"
Governor's Conference on Primary Care
Raleigh, NC
1990

"Health Care in Rural Areas"
National Rural Health Association
1991

"Rural Hospital Care"
Kentucky Hospital Association
1993

"Planning for Rural Health Care"
Southern Legislative Conference
1995

"The Need for Rural Physicians"
American Osteopathic Association Chicago, IL
1996

"Pride in Appalachia" Opening Convocation
Pikeville College
1998 "Centuries of Pride"

East Kentucky Leadership Conference
1998

"An Appalachian Story"
Morehead State University Faculty Orientation
1998

Featured in Published Articles

"Students Show Mountain Children Someone Cares" AP Nationwide News Release
1969

"Hero of the Hollow" Louisville Courier Journal
August 1, 1970

"The College with a Difference" Minutes Magazine
1970

"Students Plan to Operate 72 Health Centers" Louisville Courier Journal
1971

"Appalachia"
The New Physician magazine
1971

"Appalachia Gets a Program It Trusts" Business Week magazine
1971

"ALCOR's Key to Success in the Hollow" Editorial, Louisville Courier Journal
1971

"Their Hope - Health in the Hollow" Lexington Herald
1972

Featured in

"We Hold These Truths" Film Documentaries
American Revolution Bicentennial Committee
1973

"No Place Like Home"
WNET - New York Narrated by Helen Hays
1983

"Health Care in America"
NBC News Narrated by C. Everett Koop,
M.D. 1992

"Founding a Health Care Clinic on Faith,
Friendship, and $53" AP Nationwide News
Release
1973

"A Guide to the Up and Coming"
People magazine
1974

"New Health Care for Old Kentucky"
Modern Medicine magazine
1975

"The Metamorphosis of Benny Ray Bailey"
Ohio University Alumnus Magazine
1975

"East Kentucky's Answer-A Model for the
Future" New Physician
1976

"For These Who Serve"
New York Times
1979

Co-Producer of the Films

"And by Tomorrow"
30 minute documentary of ALCOR

"A Model for Rural Health Care"
10 minute documentary of EKHSC, Inc.

Member of

Committee for Educational Renewal for the
1970's US Department of Education
1972 -1974

Board of Directors
Mountain Comprehensive Health
1972- 1973

Administration Task Force Educational
Renewal for the 70's
1972-1973

Panel for Century Three National Science
Foundation
1974

Advisory Board
Appalachian Oral History Program
1974

Charter Member
National Committee for the Bicentennial Era
1975-1977

Chairman of the Board of Directors Kentucky
Primary Care Association, Inc. 1976-1978

Charter Member Health Committee Rural
America, Inc.
1978

Board of Directors
Regional Cluster Training Program Jackson
State University Department of Health,
Education, & Welfare
1979

Board of Directors
KY River Health Facilities Association
1982-1985

KY State Senate
1980-2000

Strategic Committee on Post-Secondary
Education
1997

Negotiated Grants

Alcoa Foundation
The Bruner Foundation
The Rockefeller Foundation
The Kellogg Foundation Western Electric Fund
DJB Foundation
The Fannie E. Rippel Foundation
The ByDale Foundation
The Robert Wood Johnson Foundation

The Edna McConnell Clark Foundation
Squibb Corporation
Bristol-Myers Foundation
Bethlehem Steel Corporation
CNA Financial Services
The Jessie Smith Noyes Foundation
The Kresge Foundation
Irwin-Sweeney-Smith Foundation
Reader's Digest Foundation
JDR III Fund
Fred Kronish Foundation
INTASA, Inc.
Joint Foundation
Mobil Oil Foundation
J. Clement & Jessie Stone Foundation
Steele-Reese Foundation
Booth Ferris Foundation
Helen E. Atwater Foundation
Florence V. Burden Foundation
Erickson Educational Foundation
The Equitable Life Assurance Society
The Merck Company Foundation
Public Welfare Foundation
Republic Steel Foundation
Schering-Plough Corporation
Warner Lambert Corporation
United States Steel Foundation
Charles and Mary Grant Foundation
Scaife Family Charitable Trusts
Morgan Guaranty Trust Company
Technicon Instruments Corporation
Department of Health and Human Services
Appalachian Regional Commission
Office of Economic Opportunity

Bibliography

Allen, Susan.
"Turner to be indicted."
The Big Sandy News. 4 May 2005.

"Appalachia gets a program it trusts."
Business Week, 16 Oct. 1971.

"ARC and Alice Lloyd College tackle rural health
problems and encourage youth
involvement through ALCOR program."
The Mountain Eagle, 10 Sep. 1970.

Bailey, Benny Ray. "Bailey praises mountains,
condemns '48 Hours.'"
Troublesome Creek Times, January 1990.

Bailey, Benny Ray.
"Negative aspects of Eastern Kentucky highlight-
ed by paper."
Lexington Herald-Leader, 28 Dec. 1990.

Bailey, Benny Ray.
"Studying Appalachia—from Lexington."
The Courier- Journal, 24 Dec. 2001.

"Bailey Bill to Spur Rural MD Practice."
The Floyd County Times, 5 March 1980.

"Bailey speaks at Pikeville College convocation."
Appalachian News- Express, 26 Aug.1998.

Baniak, Peter.
"Vote hauling played role in senate races." Lexington Herald-Leader, 29 June 2000.

"Bethlehem Steel Corporation to Contribute Up to $10,000 to the Eastern Kentucky Health Services." Knott County News, Vol. 5 No. 7, 26 April 1973.

"A Bicentennial Declaration."
Time Magazine, 3 March 1975: 24-25.

Breed, Allen G.
"E. Kentuckians want candidates' attention."
Lexington Herald-Leader, 15 May 1995.

Caudill, Charlotte H.
"Bailey-Stumbo building dedicated."
Troublesome Creek Times, 25 Aug. 2004.

C. Everett Koop, M.D. Prod. Philip Burton, Jr. Narr. C. Everett Koop.
MacNeil/Lehrer Productions, 1991. DVD.

Clifford, Gary. "Medics: Dr. Grady Stumbo and Benny Bailey go home again to build a clinic in the Appalachian Hills."
People Magazine, Vol. 12 No. 10, 3 Sep. 1979: 57-61.

Cooper, Bob.
"Clinic Cares for Hill People."
Hospital Tribune, 12 Nov. 1973. Cooper, Bob.

"Knott County health clinic: A model for entire nation."
The Sun-Telegram, 5 Jan. 1974.

"County gets 'surprise' windfall in gas taxes."
The Floyd County Times, 22 Jan.1986.
Cross, Al.

"Candidate's fund raising jumped in last weeks."
The Courier- Journal, 28 June 2000.
Cross, Al.

"Three races may influence who controls state Senate."
The Courier- Journal, 17 May 2000.

Daley, Ron. "Bailey's health care reform act is historic."
Troublesome Creek Times, Vol. 10
No. 43, 4 April 1990.

Davis, Ralph B. "Bailey denies being coup mastermind."
Paintsville Herald, Vol. 96 No. 22, 6 Jan. 1993.

Ellers, Fran.
"It's ethics or else, Stumbo warns lawmakers."
The Courier-Journal. 31 Jan. 1993.

Ellers, Fran.
"Raising coal counties' share of severance tax called possible."
The Courier-Journal. 22 Aug. 1991.

Franklin, Ben A. "Stumbo, Bailey Win Rockefeller Service Awards."
The Lexington Herald, 6 Dec. 1978.

Garrett, Robert T.
"And now, a look at business not as usual."
The Courier-Journal, 22 Oct. 1995.

Garrett, Robert T.
"Mountain Robin Hood takes on governor."
The Courier-Journal, 15 March 1998.

Gerth, Joseph. "
Bailey's defeat a signal of change."
The Courier-Journal, 28 May 2000.

Gil, Gideon.
"ABC again aims camera at irate Humana tonight."
The Courier-Journal, 15 Aug. 1991.

Gish, Tom.
"Effort to insure working poor faces obstacles."
The Mountain Eagle, 9 Jan. 1991.

"Grady Stumbo, M.D."
The Courier-Journal Magazine, 22 March 1981: 8-15, 42-43.

Graves, George.
"Mountaineer freshmen show how to climb fast in state Senate."
The Louisville Times, 15 Jan. 1980.

Hatmaker, Louise B.
"Sen. Bailey says now's the time to groom leadership."
The Jackson Times, 13 May 1993.

Hawpe, David W.
"Where are they now? East Kentucky activists aren't gone—or forgetting."
The Courier-Journal, 9 Feb. 1977.

Holwerk, David.
"Coal counties may make deal for bigger chunk of severance tax."
Lexington Herald-Leader, 30 Jan. 1980.

Indiana State University.
"Four named Distinguished Alumni."
ISU Quarterly, Vol. 7 No. 3, Fall 1980.

Jones, Karen Joy.
"Bailey chosen Person of the Year."
Troublesome Creek Times, 6 Jan. 1999.

Langfitt, Frank.
"Kentucky's Innovative Plan for Rural Health."
Washington Post Health, 10 July 1990.

Lawson, Gil.
"Surprise political move saved health reforms."
The Courier-Journal, 31 March 1996.

"Louisville Physician Named JC's Outstanding Young Man."
The Murray Ky. Ledger & Times, 5 Jan 1977.

Lucke, Jamie.
"New Senate remap would pit Bailey against Preston."
Lexington Herald-Leader, 19 Dec. 1995.

"A Promise Kept." Editorial.
The Weekly Progress, 1 April 1998.

Samples, Karen.
"Centers give torn people place to mend." Lexington Herald-Leader, 22 Feb. 1996.

"Sen. Bailey emphasizes pride in Appalachia in convocation at Lees."
The Floyd County Times, 15 April 1981.

"State Senator Benny Ray Bailey to receive honorary doctorate from Ohio University."
The Paintsville Herald, 7 April 1999.

Straub, Bill. "Bailey's 'bird bill' an attempt to make point about Eastern Kentucky culture."
The Kentucky Post,

"Times Man of the Year."
Troublesome Creek Times, 2 Jan. 1991.

Wilson, Richard and Richard Whitt.
"Senate approves bill to extend severance tax to all minerals."
The Courier-Journal, 29 March 1980.

Wolfe, Charles.
"Crafty operator: Benny Ray Bailey knows how to work a committee."
The State Journal, 4 Feb. 1990.

Yasgur, Stevan S.
"'Hillbilly clinic' brings a new brand of care to old Kentucky."
<u>Modern Medicine</u>, 15 Sep. 1975.

www.ingramcontent.com/pod-product-compliance
Lightning Source LLC
LaVergne TN
LVHW041215080426
835508LV00011B/963